Best Easy Day Hikes
Riverside

Help Us Keep This Guide Up to Date

Every effort has been made by the author and editors to make this guide as accurate and useful as possible. However, many things can change after a guide is published—trails are rerouted, regulations change, facilities come under new management, etc.

We would love to hear from you concerning your experiences with this guide and how you feel it could be improved and kept up to date. While we may not be able to respond to all comments and suggestions, we'll take them to heart and we'll also make certain to share them with the author. Please send your comments and suggestions to the following address:

The Globe Pequot Press
Reader Response/Editorial Department
P.O. Box 480
Guilford, CT 06437

Or you may e-mail us at:

editorial@GlobePequot.com

Thanks for your input, and happy trails!

Best Easy Day Hikes Series

Best Easy Day Hikes
Riverside

Allen Riedel

FALCONGUIDES®

GUILFORD, CONNECTICUT
HELENA, MONTANA

AN IMPRINT OF THE GLOBE PEQUOT PRESS

FALCONGUIDES®

Copyright © 2009 by Morris Book Publishing, LLC

Falcon, FalconGuides, and Outfit Your Mind are registered trademarks of Morris Book Publishing, LLC.

Maps created by Offroute Inc. © Morris Book Publishing, LLC

Library of Congress Cataloging-in-Publication Data
Riedel, Allen.
  Best easy day hikes, Riverside / Allen Riedel.
      p. cm. – (FalconGuides)
  ISBN 978-0-7627-5255-3
 1. Hiking–California–Riverside Region–Guidebooks. 2. Trails–California–Riverside Region–Guidebooks. 3. Riverside Region (Calif.)–Guidebooks. I. Title.
  GV199.42.C22R58 2009
  796.5109794'97–dc22

                                                    2009003238

Printed in the United States of America

10 9 8 7 6 5 4 3 2 1

Contents

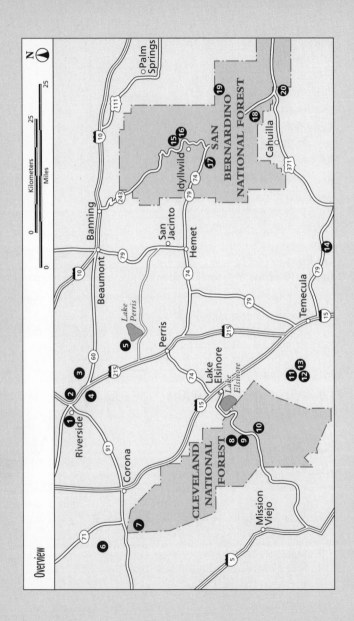
Overview

Acknowledgments

I would like to first and foremost thank all the people who have spent time hiking with me in the mountains, deserts, hills, forests, jungles, and coastal beaches. Many of you, my friends, have inspired me in countless ways, and I can't thank you enough. I would like to mention some of you by name: Sean Coolican, Adam Mendelsohn, Cameron Alston, Bill Buck, Matt Piazza, Bruno Lucidarme, Chrissy Ziburski, Eric Walther, Bob Romano, Michael Millenheft III, Jim Zuber, Danny Suarez, Eric Romero, Donn DeBaun, Alex and Dawn Wilson, Jane Weal, and Dylan Riedel.

I would also like to acknowledge my family: Monique, Michael, Sierra, and Makaila. All four of you have spent lots of time with me on trails that were great and some "not so much" . . . I love you with all my heart.

I also owe a lot to my mom and dad, Barbara and Elmer Riedel, who raised me to believe in myself. Thanks! Thanks to my brother, Larry; my grandparents, Herbert and Vivian Ward; Lucille Riedel; and my in-laws, Anna and Richard Chavez. I am a better person because of all of you.

I am also grateful for the opportunities I have been granted by writing for the most amazing Web site: www .localhikes.com. Jim Zuber has been my biggest resource into the writing world, and I can never thank him enough for the awesome site and the amount of work he has sent my way. You rule, Jim!

I would like to thank Dave Ammenheuser and Patricia Mays at the *Riverside Press Enterprise,* who have been great editors and incredible people to work for.

I would like to thank Scott Adams and the wonderful people at The Globe Pequot Press. And thanks to my other publisher, The Mountaineers Books; Ashley, Kate, Carol, and everyone there have always been spectacular.

I would also like to thank Scott Ammons and everyone at REI. It has been great getting started as an Outdoor School instructor.

Lastly, I would like to thank all the students and teachers I have worked with over the past ten years. It has been great knowing all of you.

Map Legend

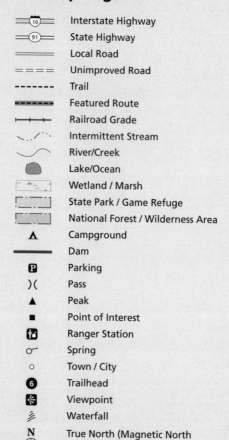	Interstate Highway
	State Highway
	Local Road
	Unimproved Road
	Trail
	Featured Route
	Railroad Grade
	Intermittent Stream
	River/Creek
	Lake/Ocean
	Wetland / Marsh
	State Park / Game Refuge
	National Forest / Wilderness Area
	Campground
	Dam
	Parking
	Pass
	Peak
	Point of Interest
	Ranger Station
	Spring
	Town / City
	Trailhead
	Viewpoint
	Waterfall
	True North (Magnetic North is approximately 15.5° East)

Introduction

This guide presents twenty easy day hikes situated in and around Riverside County, California. Located in a variety of settings ranging from county, city, and/or local parks to state parks and national forests, these are the best short hikes in the region. They cover a vast range of scenery, historical interest, and natural beauty.

Some of the best hiking in Southern California exists within a thirty- to ninety-minute drive from the city of Riverside proper. This guide is intended to be a sampling of the region that introduces families, beginning hikers, and those with only a short amount of time or energy to the incredible wonders the area has to offer.

Unknown to many outside the region, Riverside County contains a great deal of austere and captivating pastoral beauty—from the chaparral-covered slopes of the Santa Ana Mountains to the lush forests of the San Jacinto and Santa Rosa Ranges. Numerous nature preserves, reserves, and specially designated parks—ranging from the verdant Santa Rosa Plateau to the deserts of Anza-Borrego Desert State Park and Joshua Tree National Park (covered in *Best Easy Day Hikes Joshua Tree*)—protect valuable ecosystems and wildlife.

The county is named for the Santa Ana River, which flows from the highest reaches of the San Bernardino Mountains through the county and city proper past Corona and into Orange County. The water has crafted and created the landscape around the region. Many smaller creeks and tributaries feed the waterway as it flows on its way toward the Pacific Ocean.

Riverside County is the eleventh most populous county in the United States. With a total populace of more than two million, it surpasses sixteen states, all five territories, and the District of Columbia. In total area the county outranks Connecticut, Delaware, Rhode Island, and Puerto Rico—a massive region that's ripe for exploration.

Hiking is a popular activity in the region, especially in the early morning and evening during summertime and throughout the day during the rest of the year. Depending on the location, summer days can be pleasant at higher elevations—and absolutely desiccating in lower climes. Many summer hikers hit the trail in the early morning and evening to avoid the heat.

Flora and Fauna

Typically Southern Californian, the Riverside region is an arid desert ecosystem, ringed by the mountains uplifted from the tectonic forces of the San Andreas Fault. Semiarid seasonal creekside habitats and riparian canyons dot the landscape and are inhabited by varied species of mammals, reptiles, and amphibians.

The region's flora—mostly desert chaparral—can be magnificent in color, especially during certain times of the year and after a significant rainfall. Oak and pine forests grow into the higher elevations. More than forty-nine endangered species inhabit the county, including the majestic desert bighorn sheep.

Mammals abound in the mountainous regions, with black bears and mule deer inhabiting the higher reaches. Mountain lions and coyotes prowl throughout most of the county. These predators don't really present much of a danger, and their habitat is not as threatened here as in other areas of Southern California. Smaller creatures, including possums and rodents such as squirrels, skunks, mice, and the endangered kangaroo rat, inhabit the lower desert regions.

There are several large bodies of water in the region. The Salton Sea serves as a major stopping point along the Pacific Flyway, making Riverside a spectacular place for bird watching. The region's mostly man-made lakes offer both sanctuary and fishing, and more than 400 species of birds can be spotted throughout the year.

Typically the only animals in the region dangerous to humans are rattlesnakes, and during hotter months they can be prevalent on certain trails. Do not walk through tall grasses or place hands and feet anywhere before looking. Snakes understand the world by sensing vibrations and usually will be alerted and flee long before a human approaches on the trail. Rattlesnakes will only strike if they feel threatened, so if you encounter one, the best thing to do is back away or give it a wide berth on the trail.

Insects are not normally a problem in Riverside County, although ticks can present a small problem after rains, as can mosquitoes and other pests. A mild insect repellent should do the trick for most hikes, and dogs should be protected with proper vaccinations and medications.

Weather

Riverside County is mostly desert, and the lower elevations can be stifling June through September. Heat can be a factor any time of the year, although October through May is generally mild even in the hottest parts of the county.

Rain is not the normal state of affairs in Southern California. Classified as desert, Riverside County typically gets between 10 and 12 inches of rain annually. The county's rainy season is November through February, with showers more likely during December and January. Most rainstorms are over as quickly as they begin, although the region does see periods of continuing rainfall during winter.

The mountains present an entirely different climate and create weather patterns that are separate from the rest of the region. Although rainfall is rare elsewhere in the region during summer, thunderstorms can be a common occurrence in the highest elevations.

Summer temperatures can reach triple digits, although the higher mountain ranges rarely reach above the 80s. The best times of year to hike in Riverside outside the mountains are fall through spring, when temperatures are mild during the day. Early morning and evening are pleasant in the summer almost anywhere.

Preparing for Your Hike

Before you go hiking, always be prepared. Let someone know where you are planning to go, and leave an itinerary of your hiking destination with a reliable friend. Provide an expected return time and the name of the trailhead, along with specific routes you are taking. Be sure that your friend will contact authorities should you not return as expected.

Water is essential in desert environments. Hydrate before you set out and during your hike, and leave extra water in the vehicle so that you may rehydrate upon return. A good rule of thumb for hiking is one half to one liter of water per hour of hiking. On hot days without shade, you should drink as much as one gallon of water per hour of hiking and avoid overexertion during the hottest part of the day. Salty snacks can help aid water retention.

When you hike, you should always bring along the so-called "Ten Essentials"—the basic necessities for survival should the unexpected occur. Although hiking is a relatively safe activity, especially when care is taken, it is always best to prepare for any eventuality. Minor mishaps like taking a wrong turn, getting back after dark, or being lost for a short while can be frightening, but as long as cool heads prevail, most outdoor problems can be easily rectified. The following essentials are designed to keep you safe and provide a backup plan should something go wrong.

1. Navigation (map, compass, GPS)
2. Sun protection (hat, sunscreen)
3. Insulation (layered clothing)
4. Illumination (head lamp, flashlight)
5. First-aid supplies (Band-Aids, bandages, gauze, tape, tweezers, etc.)
6. Repair kit and tools (knife, duct tape, etc.)
7. Nutrition (extra food)
8. Hydration (extra water)
9. Emergency shelter (tarp, tent, sleeping bag, or emergency blanket)
10. Fire starter (for life-threatening emergencies only) NOTE: Riverside County is extremely arid, and wildfire is a constant threat. Fires are not permitted in parks, forests, and hiking areas except for designated campgrounds and yellow-post campsites. In a life-threatening emergency, clear an area 8 feet in diame-

ter around the fire and construct a rock ring to contain the fire itself. Lighting a fire outside designated areas is neither recommended nor endorsed by this guide.

This is only a basic list, and of course other items may also be useful. Spending more time on the trail will allow for individual modification to this basic list. You may find that some items are more important to you than others.

Clothing, Footwear, and Other Gear

Clothing should be worn in layers to protect your body from the elements, whether wind, heat, rain, or cold. An insulating layer of water- and sweat-wicking fabric (polyester, neoprene, polypropylene, or other synthetic fiber) is best for a basic layer. These fabrics wick sweat away from your body and keep you warm. On hot days cotton can be a good choice; the sweat will remain on the fabric, keeping you cooler than a synthetic material. Cotton is a bad choice for cold and rainy days, however—the material retains water and loses its ability to insulate, which in extreme circumstances can lead to hypothermia.

Because the material is lightweight and dries quickly, a fleece shell is good for an insulating layer. On days without a hint of precipitation, a fleece jacket may be the only outerwear you need.

Lastly, bring along a lightweight rain shell. Rain and snow can be deadly in the mountains, and a waterproof shell and pants offer protection from the elements.

Footwear

Improvements in lightweight hiking boots and shoes over the past decade have revolutionized the sport. Boots no longer need to be bulky, heavy, cumbersome Frankenstein monster–like appendages that cause blisters, chafing, and sore feet. Today many outdoor specialty shops can measure a hiker's feet and find a great-fitting shoe that can be worn immediately on the trail. These shoes are durable and sturdy, making them excellent for short day hikes, although they may not be ideal for longer and more difficult trekking.

Socks made of wool, synthetic materials, or wool-synthetic blends are best; they take moisture away from the feet, reducing chafing and blisters.

Other Gear
Backpacks for day hiking should be small, fit comfortably, and carry ten to twenty pounds. There's really no need to carry more than twenty pounds on a day hike, and doing so will probably only serve to make your experience less enjoyable. In today's ultra-light market, weeklong back-packing trips can be made carrying only twenty to twenty-five pounds (water and food included), so find a backpack that is large enough to carry what you need, but light enough to be comfortable.

Hydration systems have become the norm, and drinking from a reservoir tube is pure bliss compared to the days of cumbersome canteens or having to stop to retrieve water bottles from a pack.

Trail Regulations and Restrictions

Trails in this guide are located in national forests; preserves; and local, city, and state parks.

National forest trails require an Adventure Pass for park-ing. Adventure Passes can be purchased at sporting goods stores, specialty outdoor shops, and in the local mountains.

California state parks require a day-use entry fee, although yearly passes are available for access to all state parks. Some city parks and natural areas are free; others require day-use fees. Fees for trailhead usage are not required anywhere in Riverside County, although camping permits will most likely carry fees.

How to Use This Guide

The at-a-glance information at the beginning of each hike
includes a short description, the hike distance in miles
and type of trail (loop, lollipop or out and back), the time
required for an average hiker, elevation gain, the trail surface, the best season for hiking the trail, other trail users,
whether dogs are allowed on the hike, applicable fees or
permits, maps, and trail contacts for additional information.
Directions to the trailhead are also provided, along with
a general description of what you'll see along the way. A
detailed route finder sets forth mileages between significant
landmarks along the trail.

Maps

Easy-to-follow maps are provided for each hike. All the
hikes in this book also are covered by TOPO! CD: California CD 10 and the detailed topographic maps published by
the U.S. Geological Survey (USGS).

Greater Riverside Metropolitan Area

Historically Riverside County has been a rural region. Communities with names like Canyon Crest, Woodcrest, Edgemont, Box Springs, and more have now become ensconced into the cityscape. Newcomers to the region would have difficulty telling these areas apart. But as a consequence, the city of Riverside is loaded with parks and other outdoor spaces that remain from the merger of these communities. Parcels of land in between were left for the benefit of all who live in the area.

City, county, and private land purchases have created wilderness parks and outdoor havens prime for nearly every sort of recreational activity. Open spaces dot the cityscape.

Until the middle of the twentieth century, most of the county was a sparsely inhabited open desert dotted with citrus groves irrigated by the Santa Ana River. Not much has changed. The county is still thinly inhabited in relation to its massive land area, but the total population has increased twentyfold since the 1940s, and the population within the city itself has more than doubled since 1990.

The urban center has grown so substantially that many areas of Riverside once lined with trees have become fields of housing developments and strip malls. Regions connected by tiny dirt roads little more than a few decades ago now have arterial thoroughfares that rush an onslaught of commuters back and forth. The citrus groves of yore are almost completely gone.

The land itself is rocky and arid. Seasonal arroyos drain into the Santa Ana river basin and carry life and water during the wettest parts of the year. Rocky outcroppings like Box Springs Mountain and Mount Rubidoux provide great means of getting above it all to survey the landscape. Other urban parks are great places for idling away the time or getting away for a family stroll.

1 Mount Rubidoux Trail

This family-, bike-, and dog-friendly trail goes up through a beautiful wilderness park in the heart of the city of Riverside. The hike offers the choice of a longer, steadier climb or a shorter but steeper trip. The entire region can be surveyed from the top, which is adorned with a lovely castlelike tower and flag.

Distance: 3.5-mile lollipop
Approximate hiking time: 2 to 3 hours
Difficulty: Easy
Elevation gain: 450 feet
Trail surface: Pavement and dirt
Best season: Fall through spring; evenings or mornings in summer
Other trail users: Bikes, dogs, runners, rock climbers
Canine compatibility: Leashed

dogs permitted
Fees and permits: No fees or permits required
Maps: TOPO! CD: California CD 10; USGS: Riverside West
Trail contacts: Friends of Mount Rubidoux, 3839 Brockton Avenue, Riverside (mailing address: P.O. Box 206, Riverside 92502); (951) 683-3436; www.mt-rubidoux.org

Finding the trailhead: From Highway 91 south take the Mission Inn exit. Turn right off the ramp and proceed west on Mission Inn Boulevard for 1 mile to Redwood Drive. Turn left onto Redwood and drive 0.2 mile. Turn right onto Ninth Street and travel to the Mount Rubidoux Regional Park entrance. GPS: N33 59.11 / W117 23.10

The Hike

The Mount Rubidoux Trail is a fantastic getaway right within the Riverside city limits. The trail itself is an old road that has been locked and gated and made accessible only to

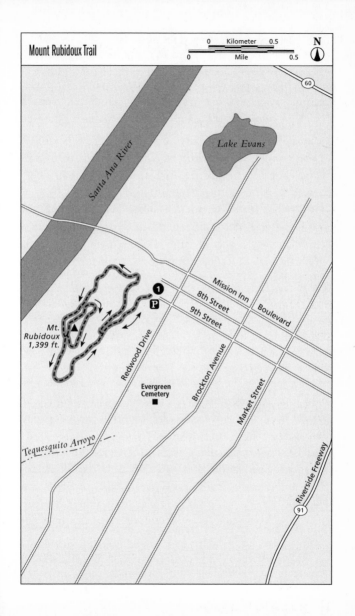

Mount Rubidoux Trail

Santa Ana River

Lake Evans

60

Mt.
Rubidoux
1,399 ft.

Mission Inn Boulevard

8th Street

9th Street

1

P

Redwood Drive

Brockton Avenue

Market Street

Evergreen
Cemetery

Tequesquito Arroyo

Riverside Freeway

91

N

Kilometer

Mile

0   0.5

pedestrians and bicyclists. The road contours around the prominent hillside and wraps the summit in a large loop. Hikers can enjoy a quick and steep 1.25-mile outing to the summit or follow the more gradual 2.25-mile ascent to the top.

Mount Rubidoux Regional Park is a shining gem that is easily and readily accessible to everyone in the general Riverside vicinity. People from all over the urban area escape to the park for a quick jog, a chance to walk their dog, a cardiovascular trail run, or a controlled bike ride.

In only a few short minutes, hikers begin to climb high above the city and leave behind the hustle and bustle of traffic-clogged streets and the stinging cacophony of the urban throng. The summit of Mount Rubidoux, a prominent mile-long plateau that sits 500 feet above the banks of the Santa Ana River, is visible from anywhere in the city.

The first 0.5 mile of the paved trail is shaded by eucalyptus and other trees planted by early homeowners along the lower section of the mount. Gradually the arbors and shadows disappear, leaving the cacti and arid desert chaparral indicative of the region. At the 0.5-mile marker, the trail splits. Turning right leads to the more gradual and longer path; continuing straight heads up the steeper and shorter trail to the top. This description follows the right-hand path.

The trail is primarily a magnet for recreation and exercise, but the park also serves as an outdoor historical museum that combines the area's history and natural resources into a unique experience. A series of plaques detailing aspects of the region are posted along the trail; one near the top points out the city's landmarks.

Views from the trail are spectacular. The entire greater Riverside area is visible, with panoramic views extending into the San Bernardino, Santa Ana, and San Gabriel Mountains. On the clearest of days, some claim that even the Pacific Ocean can be spotted glistening from the western sun in the brightest shades of blue.

The property was historically part of Jurupa Rancho, owned by Louis Robidoux. Frank Miller, of Mission Inn fame, bought the property in the early 1900s and installed the road that runs to the top. Soon after, he erected a cross at the summit. President Taft visited the summit in October 1909. In 1925 the Peace Tower and bridge were constructed in honor of Miller. The castlelike structure can be seen from the trail, inspiring children of all ages to fantasy-filled reverie.

Bicycles, strollers, and dogs are all allowed. Dogs must be on-leash, and owners are required to clean up after their pets. Cleanup bags are even provided in dispensers at the start of the trail. Cyclists must be cautious and obey the posted speed limit, as the mountain is heavily traveled.

The Friends of Mount Rubidoux is a nonprofit organization that has worked for well over a decade to make the area a safe and pleasurable place to visit and recreate. Their mission is simple and precise, with three guidelines: to restore, preserve, and beautify Mount Rubidoux Park; to enhance knowledge of the park's rich history; and to foster enjoyment by visitors to the park.

Miles and Directions

0.0 Start walking on the paved trail beyond the gated entrance to Mount Rubidoux Regional Park at Ninth Street and Mount Rubidoux Drive.

0.5 The trail intersects an unsigned loop. Bear right and climb for 1.5 miles as the trail wraps around the mountainside.

2.0 The trail reaches a bridge and a three-way intersection. Cross up and over the bridge for the upper loop, and head toward the summit. You'll return here after viewing the sights at the top. (Options: Going straight under the bridge leads to the upper loop and Peace Tower. Turning right heads down 1.0 mile back to the first trail intersection.)

3.0 Reach an unsigned Y junction. Continue straight and hike down to the main gate.

3.5 Arrive back at trailhead.

2 University of California, Riverside, Botanic Gardens

This is a shady and beautiful walk through a lush canyon where the University of California showcases trees and plants from all over California, the eastern United States, Australia, China, and South Africa.

Distance: 0.5-mile lollipop
Approximate hiking time: 30 minutes to 2 hours
Difficulty: Easy
Elevation gain: 70 feet
Trail surface: Asphalt and compacted dirt
Best season: Fall through spring; evening or morning in summer
Other trail users: Wheelchairs, strollers
Canine compatibility: No dogs allowed

Fees and permits: Parking, plus a suggested donation
Maps: TOPO! CD: California CD 10; USGS: Riverside East
Trail contacts: Curator, Botanic Gardens, University of California, Riverside 92521-0124; (951) 784-6962; www.gardens.ucr .edu; e-mail, Friends of the UCR Botanic Gardens: ucrbg@ucr.edu

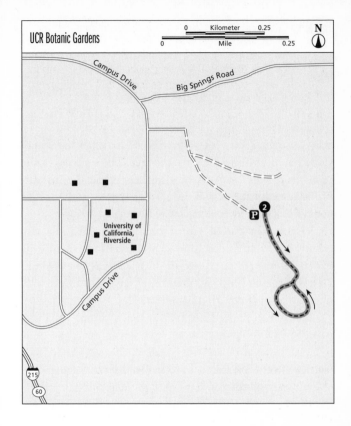

Finding the trailhead: From Interstate 215 South-Highway 60 east, exit at Martin Luther King Boulevard and turn right. Drive 0.2 mile on Martin Luther King, and turn right onto Canyon Crest. Canyon Crest ends at West Campus Drive. Turn right onto West Campus Drive, and follow the signs as the road curves around campus for 0.75 mile to reach the cedar-lined drive to the garden entrance and parking area. The right turn for Lot 13 is just before Big Springs Road. GPS: N33 58.17 / W117 19.12

The Hike

Beautiful, wooded, and green, the botanic gardens at the University of California silhouette forty acres of wild mountainous topography on the eastern borders of the city of Riverside. Lodged beneath Box Springs Mountain, the gardens are a tranquil little slice of paradise crisscrossed by more than 4.0 miles of trail. Two verdant arroyos, Alder and Chancellor's Canyons, meander through the preserve. The gardens contain more than 3,500 varieties of plant life. While the majority of the flora is native Californian, some species in the garden come from as far away as Africa and Australia.

Visitors can purchase brochures at the gatehouse that outline four self-guided tours. The gardens are open daily 8:00 a.m. to 5:00 p.m., except on Christmas, New Year's Day, Independence Day, and Thanksgiving. Admission is free, but a small donation is suggested.

A free map displays the various routes through the gardens. Several routes loop around on one another, and there is no real way to "see" the gardens. Several smaller side paths split off from the main routes, and visitors can choose any number of courses. This hike presents just one option out of many.

Nearly one-third of the total terrain remains unplanted to display the chaparral grasslands and coastal scrub native to the Riverside area. The sheer diversity of plants allows for varying bloom periods throughout the year. Check with the gatehouse visitor center or call ahead to find out what is blossoming when you plan to visit.

From the entrance gate, this hike begins in Alder Canyon—and naturally, alders line the entrance. A peaceful and seasonal creek flows through the lovely glen. Ascending upward from the entrance, hikers and visitors in wheelchairs can enjoy hilltop vistas that overlook Riverside County, Box Springs Mountain, and wide-ranging views of the San Bernardino Mountains.

Follow the gently graded and paved wheelchair-accessible path to tour the brightest spots of the gardens, including Alder Canyon, Lilac Lane, and the rose, herb, and iris gardens. These special sections were landscaped to allow visitors to view specific species within one particular area. Some of the collections are arranged by region; others are grouped by classification.

People of all ages and families are encouraged to visit. Most of the main path is shaded, and benches line the garden pathways for respites. You could easily spend half a day ambling through the gardens or zip through in an hour or less. A free bingo game sheet is provided for children, encouraging them to find some of the flora and fauna that inhabit the gardens.

Miles and Directions

0.0 Start walking up Alder Canyon on the paved wheelchair path after entering through the turnstile.

0.1 Stay right on the paved pathway; follow the path as it loops around through the rose and iris gardens.

0.3 Turn right onto the paved roadway to return to the trailhead. (**Option:** A spur trail heads left and leads to a greenhouse and a restroom. Both paved routes return to Alder Canyon.)

0.5 Arrive back at the entrance.

3 Sycamore Canyon Wilderness Park

Sycamore Canyon Wilderness Park is a mecca for outdoor enthusiasts in the Riverside region. A network of trails criss-cross and intersect, enabling the creation of multiple routes/trails of varying lengths. Three park entrances offer easy access to the undeveloped landscape.

Distance: 2.5-mile loop
Approximate hiking time: 1.5 hours
Difficulty: Easy
Elevation gain: 400 feet
Trail surface: Dirt trail
Best season: Fall through spring; evening or morning in summer
Other trail users: Bicycles, horses, dogs

Canine compatibility: Leashed dogs permitted
Fees and permits: No fees or permits required
Maps: TOPO! CD: California CD 10; USGS: Riverside East
Trail contacts: Sycamore Canyon Wilderness Park, 600 Central Avenue, Riverside 92507; (951) 826-2000; www.riversideca.gov/park_rec/amenities.asp

Finding the trailhead: From Interstate 215 south/Highway 60 east, exit at Central Avenue. Turn right and drive for 0.75 mile to the park entrance. Turn left into the large dirt parking area. GPS: N33 57.16 / W117 19.17

The Hike

Located between Riverside and Moreno Valley at the junction of Highway 60 and I-215, Sycamore Canyon is a beautiful, untamed nature reserve. The 1,550-acre park is a prime location for hiking, biking, and horseback riding. More than 12 miles of trails cross the rugged, chaparral-

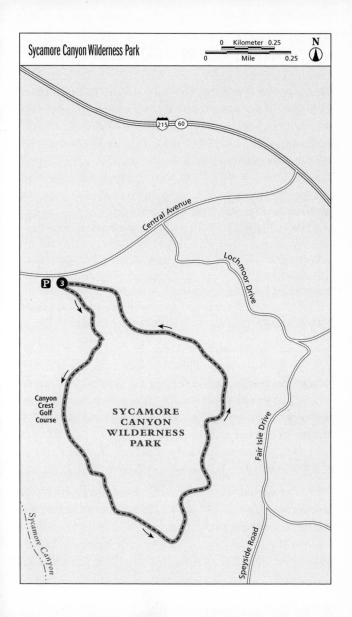

Sycamore Canyon Wilderness Park

0 Kilometer 0.25
0 Mile 0.25

N

215 60

Central Avenue

Lochmoor Drive

P 3

Canyon
Crest
Golf
Course

SYCAMORE
CANYON
WILDERNESS
PARK

Fair Isle Drive

Sycamore Canyon

Speyside Road

covered landscape, providing a quick getaway from the urban atmosphere of Riverside proper.

The park is open from thirty minutes after sunrise until thirty minutes before sunset, but the best time for a stroll is early morning or later in the evening, especially when the day is hot. There is not much shade to be had in this arid landscape, although lush canyon habitats do provide for taller trees in some of the park's recesses. Since the park is highly exposed to the sun, it is always important to carry an ample supply of water. Drinking fountains are located at the main entrance at 400 Central Avenue.

The broad and well-defined trails are used daily by runners, equestrians, people with dogs, and mountain bikers. Improvements are constantly being planned and implemented, including updated information kiosks, signs, and trail markers.

The sounds of the surrounding city are noticeable in most parts of the park. However, Sycamore Canyon is a very large and open space that deposits hikers far enough away to create a feeling of placidity and calm along the trail. It is a great place for introducing children to the natural world, and if there isn't any smog, it feels like an escape into the backwoods—even though cell phones have reception almost everywhere in the region.

Wildlife is plentiful in the park, which also serves as a preserve for the endangered Stephens' kangaroo rat and California gnatcatcher. The landscape and several of its inhabitants are federally protected by various agencies. Creatures such as chuckwallas, burrowing owls, red-tailed hawks, jackrabbits, desert cottontails, mourning doves, turkey vultures, coyotes, and the western diamondback rattlesnake all reside within the park.

The hike follows a well-defined loop through the park, although many smaller trails intersect and cut across the main trail, making it very difficult to provide accurate and precisely detailed directions. For the route described here, follow the main trail south. Turn right, staying on the most well-defined path as it ascends a ridge and continues south toward a housing development. Turn left and ascend another ridge as the trail turns northward and returns to the parking area.

Miles and Directions

0.0 Start at the parking area, and travel south along the main route through the park.

0.2 Turn right onto the most worn route, and continue beyond a lush canyon onto another ridgeline. Follow this well-traveled route southward for 1.1 miles toward a group of homes.

1.2 Near the houses on Speyside Road, turn left and follow the well-defined trail up and over canyons and ridges back toward the trailhead. The route follows a mostly northern direction from this point.

2.5 Arrive back at the parking area.

4 Box Springs Mountain Reserve

Hike along an old maintenance road to the summit of Box Springs Mountain, which overlooks the Inland Empire and the big "M" above Moreno Valley. Views extend across Southern California, and on clear days the panoramic view is sublime. Descend along a breathtaking trail that wraps around the mountainside.

Distance: 4.0-mile shuttle
Approximate hiking time: 2 hours
Difficulty: Easy
Elevation gain: 700 feet
Trail surface: Dirt road
Best season: Fall through spring; evening or morning in summer
Other trail users: Bicycles, horses, dogs
Canine compatibility: Leashed dogs permitted

Fees and permits: No fees or permits required
Maps: TOPO! CD: California CD 10; USGS: Riverside East
Trail contacts: Riverside County Parks, 9699 Box Springs Mountain Road, Moreno Valley 92557; (951) 684-7032; www.riverside countyparks.org/park-directory/all-parks/box-springs; Box Spring Reserve: http://nrs.ucop.edu/Box-Spring.htm

Finding the trailhead: From Riverside take Highway 60 east to the Pigeon Pass exit. Turn left and drive 1.9 miles north to Old Lake/Hidden Springs Drive. Turn left onto Hidden Springs and drive 0.2 mile before turning left onto a dirt road signed for Box Springs Canyon. Leave a car in the parking area and return to Pigeon Pass Road. Turn left and continue north for 1.6 miles to where Pigeon Pass curves to the left. Stay left on Pigeon Pass. At 0.4 mile continue straight where the road splits and becomes Box Springs Mountain Road. Follow Box Springs Mountain Road for 1.3 miles to the turnoff for the parking area. GPS: N33 58.51 / W117 17.23

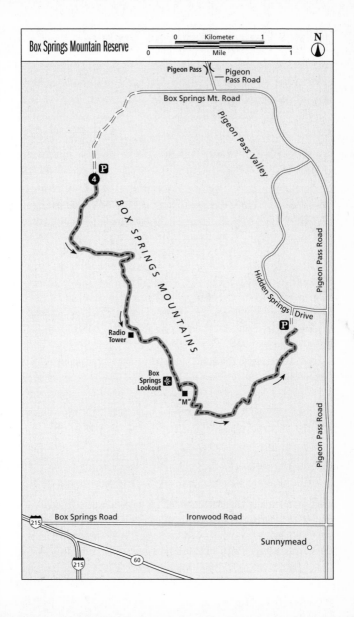

The Hike

NOTE: Although this hike is presented as a point-to-point requiring a car shuttle, it can be done as an out-and-back from either the starting or ending point.

The Box Springs Mountains dominate the northern skyline above the cities of Riverside and Moreno Valley. Some 1,150 acres of rough and untamed territory have been protected in a spacious and beautiful park and preserve that bears the mountains' name. Miles of dirt roads and trails dot the landscape, although the park itself is often overlooked and underutilized. Equestrians, mountain bikers, families, and even dogs are all welcome. Best of all, there is no entrance or day-use fee.

This hike gently climbs along a dirt road to the apex of the mountain ridge and summit of Box Springs Mountain. At the repeater towers and the overlook, the road becomes a singletrack trail and descends to the Hidden Springs entrance of the park.

Box Springs Mountain is notable for the two giant letters stamped into its side and the radio towers located atop the summit plateau. The giant poured-concrete letter "C" was placed in the west for the University of California at Riverside, although the logic behind the choice of the letter "C" may only be understood by a select few. The reasoning behind the giant "M" on the Moreno Valley side is a bit more obvious. The radio towers are enormous and can be seen from a great distance away.

Box Springs Mountain Reserve has not been tamed by civilization. True, the towers stationed along the crest demonstrate the footprint of mankind, but walking along the ridge feels amazingly wild and free. The views from on high are absolutely astounding. Vistas at the top stretch from horizon to horizon.

The range is named for a spring on the eastern side of the range. Apparently a cowboy who used the spring to water his horses noticed it had become unusable. He dug it up and fitted the sides with a wooden box, hence the name.

Hiking routes up the mountain are both steep and craggy. The most popular routes follow old roads, but there are excellent examples of steep singletrack trail for those looking for something other than the route most frequently traveled. The trail down the mountain that completes this hike is one such trail.

The park is a masterpiece of scenery. After winter rains—the best time being between February and March—the hillsides bloom in a rich hue of gold, with all the colors of the rainbow represented on a smaller scale. The flora of the region is a transitional mixture of coastal sage scrub and chamise chaparral.

Many species of reptile, mammal, and avian creatures thrive in the park. Mule deer, coyotes, bobcats, golden eagles, white-tailed kestrels, and western meadowlarks are just a few of the fauna that can be found trailside. Mountain lions also prowl the terrain. Although there have been no attacks within the park, warning signs are posted at the trailheads. Be observant and always use caution, especially with small children and pets.

Miles and Directions

0.0 Start at the trailhead on Box Springs Mountain Road, and begin hiking along the dirt road.

0.5 Veer left and continue climbing along the main roadway as it splits into two roads.

1.5 Continue straight, and take the left path that continues beyond the first set of radio repeater towers.

2.1 Take the left fork beyond the second set of radio towers.

2.2 Arrive at the summit and overlook for the big "M." Turn around and look for the trail down the mountain on the right.

2.3 Turn right and follow the trail to the Hidden Springs Parking Area.

4.0 Arrive at the Hidden Springs Parking Area and pick up your shuttle car.

Lake Perris
State Recreation Area

ituated between the suburban towns of Moreno
Valley and Perris, Lake Perris is better known for
its boating and RV camping than its hiking trails.
However, the myriad outdoor opportunities available for
those so inclined are one of the park's best-kept secrets.
Marked by the boulders and large rock outcroppings
that dot much of Riverside County, Lake Perris has a
distinctive look that's ringed by small mountains and
the Bernasconi Hills. A land of upheaval built from the
seismic activity and tectonic fault lines that run through
the region like a jigsaw puzzle, the recreation area is
starkly beautiful.

Native legends state that the rocky hillsides and large
outcroppings were caused by the demon god Tahquitz, who
lived near the upper summits of the San Jacinto Range. In
his rage, he would hurl pieces of the mountains from the sky,
leaving them to fall on the unsuspecting valleys and basin
below. Of course, the geologic processes actually involved
leave less to the imagination and more to the march of time,
uplift, and erosion; but they still have imprinted a monu-
mental and austere mark on the landscape. Visitors who take
the time to appreciate all the natural beauty here will be
thankful for that impression.

The hiking trails in Lake Perris State Recreation Area
are exquisite, remote, seldom traveled, rich in viewpoints

and wildlife, and intensely rewarding. Perfect as altitude trainers for those who live in the Riverside region or for those who wish to find an outdoor workout nearby, the high peaks can provide a cardiovascular workout regimen or a short getaway for those who wish to do either. The hike to Russell Peak can be a one-day trek or a daily warm-up for bigger and higher mountains.

Hundreds of species of birds migrate to and from the lake; hawks and owls frequently prowl the skies, hunting by day and night. The region's primary floral community is coastal sage scrub chaparral, with native grasses still surviving in some areas. Mule deer, coyotes, bobcats, roadrunners, quail, and rabbits are commonly seen throughout the area. During the rainy season, wildflowers put on an engaging and beautiful display.

5 Terri Peak Trail

This trail in beautiful Lake Perris State Recreation Area climbs a mountain overlooking a sparkling-blue lake. All of Southern California is visible from one of the most prominent vantage points in the area.

Distance: 2.6 miles out and back
Approximate hiking time: 1.5 hours
Difficulty: Easy
Elevation gain: 800 feet
Trail surface: Dirt trail
Best season: Fall through spring; evenings or mornings in summer
Other trail users: Dogs, bicycles

Canine compatibility: Leashed dogs permitted
Fees and permits: Day-use fee per vehicle; annual pass
Maps: TOPO! CD: California CD 10; USGS: Riverside East
Trail contacts: Lake Perris State Recreation Area, 17801 Lake Perris Drive, Perris 92571; (951) 940-5600; www.parks.ca .gov/?page_id=651

Finding the trailhead: From Interstate 215 south in Riverside, exit left onto the Ramona Expressway and drive for 3 miles. Turn left onto Lake Perris Drive and drive 1 mile to the entry booth. Continue 0.6 mile to the entrance for the Ya'i Heki' Regional Indian Museum. The trail begins behind the museum. GPS: N33 51.57 / W117 11.53

The Hike

This fantastic hike leads to small but majestic Terri Peak on the border of Moreno Valley and Perris. The summit is isolated and there are no higher mountains anywhere in the vicinity, making the view from the top one of the best in Southern California.

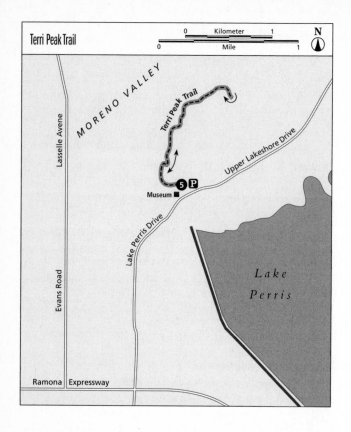

Every major mountain from Santa Monica to San Diego and much of the Los Angeles Basin can be seen on clear days, not to mention sparkling-blue Lake Perris, which seems close enough to touch. The recreation area is known more for its water sports than its hiking trails, and much of this hike is on a rarely used trail. Chances are, even on weekends you won't meet anyone else on this hike.

The trail is a no-nonsense path that leads to the top. Some small deer paths crisscross the main trail, but it is easy to tell the difference between the maintained route and the smaller game trails. As the trail nears the summit, it intersects an old road used to service the radio towers that once adorned the peak. Turn right and follow the short trail to the top.

Without a doubt, the top of Terri Peak is one of the finest spots in the Inland Empire for watching the sunset. Unearthly hues illuminate the sky, and gentle breezes always blow at day's end. Because of high summer temperatures and smog, it's best to make the ascent fall through spring. But summer evenings can provide an escape from the heat—and a fantastic workout. Dusk is a quiet and serene time along the trail.

Lake Perris State Recreation Area is a glittering gem of the Riverside metro area, and most people are unaware of the diverse recreational opportunities the lake and its almost 9,000 acres of protected parkland provide. Rattlesnakes are common and present a small danger along the trail for children and pets. Mountain lions and coyotes also roam freely, although they are rarely seen.

The shrubbery is mainly desert grasses and chaparral such as brittlebrush, buckwheat, black and white sages, and sagebrush. The upper plateau is gorgeous after the winter rains. Wildflowers flourish from November through April, including goldfields, poppies, fiddleneck, and phacelia.

The Ya'i Heki' Regional Indian Museum provides insight into Native American culture in Southern California, specifically the region's desert tribes. The museum is open Saturday and Sunday from 10:00 a.m. to 4:00 p.m. Enjoy the exhibits after a great hike.

Miles and Directions

0.0 Start behind the Ya'i Heki' Regional Indian Museum, and begin hiking on the trail to Terri Peak.

1.2 Turn right at the unsigned trail junction, and continue 0.1 mile to the summit.

1.3 Arrive at the summit of Terri Peak, and enjoy the views before retracing your steps.

1.4 Turn left at the unsigned trail junction, and return down the trail.

2.6 Arrive back at the museum.

Chino Hills
State Park

Chino Hills State Park is a magnificent swath of Southern California landscape straddling Orange, Los Angeles, and Riverside Counties. The preserve is made up of mostly old ranchlands and dotted with preexisting trails and dirt roads open to hikers, equestrians, and bicyclists. Old ranch properties and other remnants of a bygone era line the 60 miles of trails that crisscross the park. The rolling hillsides and riparian streamsides provide solace from the city and the urbanity of the Southern California Basin.

Chino Hills State Park is a conglomeration of several parks, privately acquired holdings, and land purchases that serve as a vital wildlife corridor connecting the Santa Ana Mountains in the south to the Whittier Narrows in the north and the foothills of the Angeles National Forest. The beauty of the park belies its urban nature. Despite being situated in the middle of one of the most populated regions on the planet, the park feels remote and empty. The splendor and magnificence of the preserve lie not in its diversity or a sort of wild ruggedness. Instead the homogeneity of the scenery and the gentle rolling landscapes provide a tableau that transfixes the senses on the lush hillsides and the lively canyons that cut across them.

More than 14,100 acres of prime California real estate have been protected in Chino Hills State Park. A nonprofit group called Hills for Everyone is still working to preserve other parcels of land and enlarge the park's boundaries. The park stretches for 31 miles and guards a variety of plants and wildlife, providing important ecosystems in a rapidly developing area.

6 Telegraph Canyon–South Ridge Loop

Enjoy a meandering stroll through 14,100-acre Chino Hills State Park, where rolling grasslands and groves of oaks and sycamores share history, natural preservation, and solitude. The preserve provides an open-space experience in the middle of urban Southern California.

Distance: 4.0-mile loop

Approximate hiking time: 2 hours

Difficulty: Easy

Elevation gain: 600 feet

Trail surface: Dirt road

Best season: Fall through spring; evening or morning in summer

Other trail users: Bicycles, horses

Canine compatibility: No dogs allowed

Fees and permits: Day-use fee per vehicle; annual state parks pass

Maps: TOPO! CD: California CD 10; USGS: Prado Dam

Trail contacts: Chino Hills State Park, 4721 Sapphire Road, Chino Hills (mailing address: 1879 Jackson Street, Riverside 92504); (951) 780-6222; www .parks.ca.gov/?page_id=648

Finding the trailhead: From Highway 91 in Corona, take Highway 71 north for 6.7 miles. Exit onto the Soquel Canyon Parkway and turn left. Drive on the parkway for 1.1 miles and turn left onto Elinvar Drive. Elinvar turns left and becomes Sapphire Road. Follow the signs and turn right onto Bane Canyon Road. Follow Bane Canyon for 1 mile to the entry booth. Continue 2.25 miles as the road makes a hairpin turn and arrives in the Rolling M Ranch parking area. GPS: N33 55.26 / W117 42.21

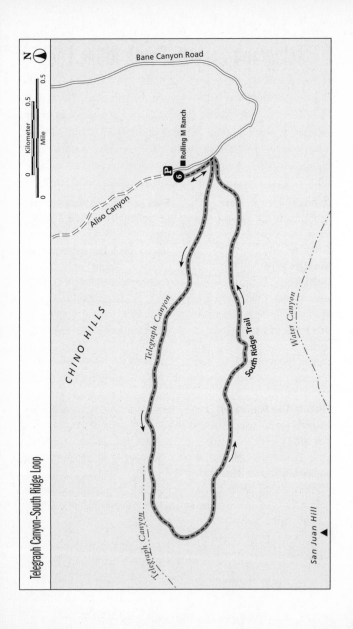

Telegraph Canyon–South Ridge Loop

Bane Canyon Road

Rolling M Ranch

Aliso Canyon

CHINO HILLS

Telegraph Canyon

South Ridge Trail

Telegraph Canyon

Water Canyon

San Juan Hill

N

0   0.5   Kilometer
0   0.5   Mile

The Hike

This lovely route travels through the heart of Chino Hills State Park, starting at Rolling M Ranch and making a 4.0-mile loop through rustic and peaceful countryside. The hills begin to turn green in January, just after the seasonal rains. A few short weeks to months later, the wildflowers are in bloom. Groves of oaks and sycamores are found in and alongside the canyons. During spring, the namesake rolling hills are verdant and green. California poppies, black mustard, toyon, fennel, and thistle are ubiquitous; morning glories and bushflowers are also plentiful.

Head south on Bane Canyon Road from the parking area, and turn right onto the gated dirt road for the Telegraph Canyon Trail. Follow the road as it ripples and undulates through the park's trademark wavy hillsides. The relatively flat old ranch and fire road follows a riparian area alongside a creek for the first 1.0 mile of the hike. The sylvan stream runs year-round in some areas. There is a good deal of shade for the first mile, but the trail eventually climbs out of the canyon and becomes sun exposed for the rest of the hike. Birds such as wrens, woodpeckers, and vireos flitter about in the trees. Western tree squirrels inhabit the same arbors and often leap from limb to limb.

In the next mile the road climbs 300 feet, curves, and intersects the South Ridge Trail, which returns east to the start of the hike. Ridgeline trails generally reward hikers with remarkable views of the surrounding countryside; this one takes in lovely vistas of the hillsides and canyons.

Other options are available for those who wish to get off the roadways. The Hills for Everyone Trail intersects at 1.0 mile and can also be followed as a loop. For those not wishing to complete the loop, a lovely viewpoint can easily serve as a turnaround spot.

Chino Hills acts as an important refuge for more than 200 species of birds, mammals, amphibians, and reptiles. These include birds such as the least Bell's vireo, California gnatcatcher, coastal cactus wren, red-tailed hawk, and turkey vulture, as well as animals like mule deer, bobcats, coyotes, and mountain lions. The park is crucial as a wildlife corridor, protecting the habitat of many Southern California plants and animals and helping ensure their survival.

Miles and Directions

0.0 Start at the Rolling M Ranch parking area, and head south on Bane Canyon Road.

0.2 Turn right onto Telegraph Canyon Road.

1.0 Continue straight on the left-hand path at the junction with the Hills for Everyone Trail.

2.0 Continue straight on the left-hand path past a small spur trail.

2.1 Turn left onto the South Ridge Trail when the Telegraph Canyon Road leads off to the right. Circle back toward the Rolling M Ranch.

2.3 Continue right and straight past a spur trail on the left.

2.5 Continue left and straight past another spur trail on the right.

3.7 Turn left onto Bane Canyon Road.

4.0 Arrive back at the parking area.

7 Coal Canyon

The hike climbs a lovely canyon that hosts an intermittent arroyo and a seasonal waterfall. The area was an important battleground for preserving Southern California's wildlife and acts as a crucial corridor for many species.

Distance: 5.6 miles out and back

Approximate hiking time: 2.5 hours

Difficulty: Easy

Elevation gain: 400 feet

Trail surface: Pavement, dirt road, dirt trail

Best season: Fall through spring; evening or morning in summer

Other trail users: None

Canine compatibility: No dogs allowed

Fees and permits: No fees or permits required

Maps: TOPO! CD: California CD 10; USGS: Black Star Canyon

Trail contacts: Chino Hills State Park, 4721 Sapphire Road, Chino Hills (mailing address: 1879 Jackson Street, Riverside 92504); (951) 780-6222; www .parks.ca.gov/?page_id=648

Finding the trailhead: From Highway 91 west in Corona, exit at Green River Road. Turn right (west) onto Green River Road and drive for 1 mile. Park in the lot on the right just before the road turns and enters the golf course. Follow Green River Road for 0.2 mile to the Santa Ana River Bike Trail. GPS: N33 52.21 / W117 39.57

The Hike

Beginning on the Santa Ana River Trail, the hike travels alongside the cement-reinforced banks of the Santa Ana River. On the north side is the Green River Golf Course; on the south is the roaring Highway 91. The path follows

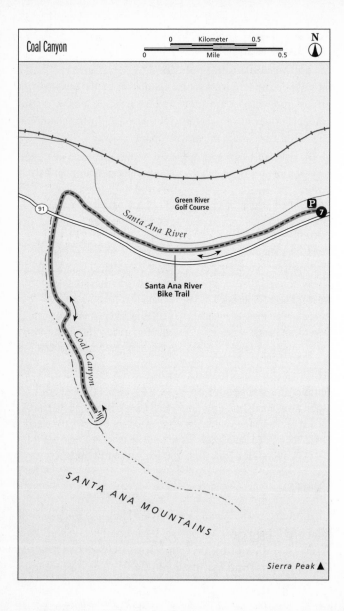

Coal Canyon

| 0 | Kilometer | 0.5 |
| 0 | Mile | 0.5 |

N

91

Green River
Golf Course

P
7

Santa Ana River

Santa Ana River
Bike Trail

Coal Canyon

SANTA ANA MOUNTAINS

Sierra Peak ▲

this route for 1.0 mile before it turns left under the overpasses and enters the wilds of Coal Canyon.

This immediate area was slated for development, housing tracts, and a freeway exit until it was discovered that the area provided a crucial gateway for wildlife in both the Chino/Puente Hills region and the Santa Ana Mountains. This one freeway underpass served as a critical link in the food chain of Southern California, and severing it would have critically impacted all wild creatures living in both the forest and the state park. After a battle, the corridor was preserved, and today creatures and hikers alike can enjoy the canyon's splendor.

From the underpass, old truck trails emerge in roughly three directions: east, west, and south. Follow the route to the south that skirts alongside the sand and gravel watershed, and hike upcanyon, staying to the left of the creek. Water flows intermittently, but the area is low in elevation. The best time to see water is during or shortly after the spring rainy season. Expect exceedingly and even dangerously hot days in summer—and not a hint of water.

The hike climbs up the shadeless canyon for 1.0 mile until the walls of the gorge begin to taper inward. Here what is left of the road ends and a trail descends into the creekbed. Follow the trail for another 0.5 mile to a splendid and tranquil hollow where a lovely 20-foot waterfall spits water over hardened calcium carbonate deposits. Expect water only in the wettest months of the year, and even then there is no guarantee.

Miles and Directions

0.0 Start at the parking lot, and walk 0.2 mile west down Green River Road to the Santa Ana River Bike Trail.

0.2 Continue west on the Santa Ana River Bike Trail for 1.0 mile.

1.2 Turn left and cross under Highway 91. (FYI: This was once a planned exit and paved underpass. The area has been returned to a natural state to serve as a wildlife corridor.)

1.3 Continue straight along the old 4x4 road as it stays along the left bank of the streambed.

2.3 The 4x4 road ends and becomes a trail that drops into the streambed. Continue for 0.5 mile to where the canyon walls narrow.

2.8 Arrive at a seasonal waterfall. Return via the same route.

5.6 Arrive back at the parking lot.

Santa Ana Mountains– Cleveland National Forest

The Santa Ana Mountains run roughly north from the Santa Ana River to the Santa Margarita and San Luis Rey Rivers in the south, dividing Orange and Riverside Counties. Foothills ebb into the Pacific Ocean in the west and taper into the Inland Valley in the east. Primarily a coastal range, the mountains are sparsely forested, vegetated mostly by coastal chaparral and sage scrub grasslands. Nonnative flora and grasses have changed the ecology of the region since the arrival of the Spanish, and frequent wildfires have altered the landscape that was still heavily forested a little more than one hundred years ago.

Today even the tops of the mountains are mostly without trees, and remaining stands of pine trees are few and far between. The hotter seasons and lower elevations coupled with invasive species have taken a toll on the woodlands. Canyons and arroyos, along with many isolated pockets, still retain their arboreal splendor under the shade of cottonwood, laurel, sycamore, walnut, ash, willow, alder, and oak. The intermittent streams and canyons in the Santa Ana Mountains are some of the most beautiful in all California.

Often magnificent, these riparian habitats sparkle, as do the clear views from on high.

Since the range is relatively low in elevation, all peaks sit below 6,000 feet, summer temperatures can be scorching. Ocean breezes do not make it very far inland, which makes the Santa Anas perfect for late fall, winter, and early spring exploration. Because most people hike solely in the summertime, there are miles upon miles of trail in the forest that go largely unvisited and underexplored.

The mountains are bordered by Highway 91 to the north and Highway 76 to the south and divided by Highway 74, which runs almost directly through the heart of the range. National forest campgrounds and visitor centers are located in the most popular areas, and an Adventure Pass is required to park in most spots throughout the region.

8 Chiquito Trail

This point-to-point shuttle hike travels downhill through a lovely wooded canyon that provides shade and solitude. The trail passes a seasonal waterfall and stream, and the views are magnificent. The easy downhill gradient makes this longer hike a great half-day outing.

Distance: 8.0-mile shuttle
Approximate hiking time: 4 hours
Difficulty: Easy
Elevation gain: 600 feet; mostly gradual downhill
Trail surface: Dirt trail
Best season: Fall through spring; evenings or mornings in summer
Other trail users: Bicycles, dogs, horses

Canine compatibility: Leashed dogs permitted
Fees and permits: Adventure Pass required
Maps: TOPO! CD: California CD 10; USGS: Alberhill, Sitton Peak
Trail contacts: Cleveland National Forest, Trabuco Ranger District, 1147 East Sixth Street, Corona; 92879; (951) 736-1811; www.fs.fed.us/r5/cleveland

Finding the trailhead: Take Interstate 15 south from Riverside and exit at Central Avenue/Highway 74 in Lake Elsinore. Turn right onto Central Avenue/Highway 74 and drive for 0.1 mile. Turn right onto Collier Avenue and drive for 0.5 mile. Turn left at Riverside Drive and go 3.2 miles. Veer left onto Grand Avenue and continue for 0.6 mile. Turn right onto Ortega Highway and continue into the mountains for 8.3 miles. Leave one car in the parking lot for the San Juan Loop Trail across from the Ortega Country Cottage Candy Store and Gift Shoppe. Head north for 1.8 miles on Ortega Highway. Turn left onto Long Canyon Road and travel north 2.4 miles to Blue Jay Campground. The trailhead is located just before the campground. GPS: N33 39.8 / W117 26.54

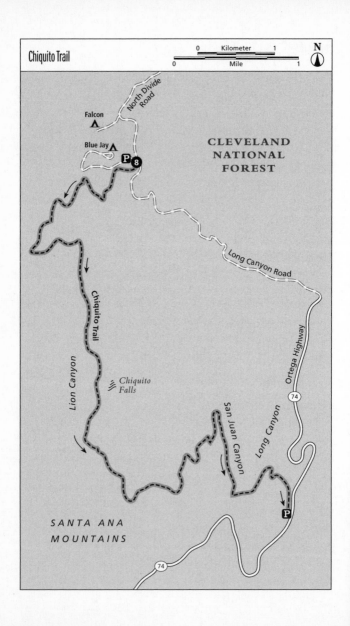

Chiquito Trail

Kilometer
0   1

Mile
0   1

N

Falcon ▲

North Divide Road

Blue Jay ▲

P 8

CLEVELAND
NATIONAL
FOREST

Long Canyon Road

Chiquito Trail

Lion Canyon

Chiquito Falls

San Juan Canyon

Long Canyon

Ortega Highway

74

SANTA ANA
MOUNTAINS

P

74

74

The Hike

The Chiquito Trail is a wonderful way to take a longer hike with the difficulty rating still set in the easy category. The way to do it is by traveling downhill almost all the way. The trail starts high up in the Santa Ana Mountains and descends through a shady wooded canyon for most of the route. High mountain vistas appear all along the hike and the scenery is superb, especially if you take the hike after the rains, when the land is colorful and in full bloom. Spring hikers can expect to see a virtual rainbow of wildflowers along the trail, including red and yellow monkeyflower, toyon, ceanothus, California poppies, black mustard, and wild blackberries.

To begin the hike, take the San Juan Trail from Blue Jay Campground and follow it for 1.8 miles to the junction with the Chiquito Trail. Turn left and continue downhill through lovely Lion Canyon. There are several trail crossings and junctions in the first 2.0 miles, but they are well marked and well used. Water generally flows from winter through early summer in wetter years, and the scenery is sheltered from the sun by sycamores and gigantic oaks that are hundreds of years old.

At the halfway point, the trail leaves Lion Canyon and ascends the ridgeline below the unnamed 2,800-foot summit to the east. If the water is flowing through Lion Canyon, you'll see and hear lovely and idyllic Chiquito Falls cascading over a large rocky ledge. From here the trail grows substantially less forested and travels through coastal chaparral and outcroppings of sun-kissed boulders for the remainder of the trip.

Wrapping around the aforementioned summit, the trail descends into another canyon and eventually intersects the

San Juan Loop after 7.0 miles of hiking. Either direction is 1.0 mile to the parking lot, with the right-hand path gaining slightly more elevation to reach the roadway. Turn left and enjoy the rest of the route to the car shuttle.

Option: San Juan Canyon usually has water with pools and creekbeds suitable for wading. The short loop around the canyon is a favorite of families and people making stops along the highway.

Miles and Directions

0.0 Start hiking south on the San Juan Trail adjacent to the east end of the campground.

1.2 There are four trail crossings within the next 0.5 mile. Stay on the San Juan Trail until it intersects the Chiquito Trail.

1.8 Head left on the Chiquito Trail, and hike into Lion Canyon.

4.0 Pass Chiquito Falls and climb an unnamed ridge.

6.0 Drop into upper San Juan Canyon and turn south toward the San Juan Loop.

7.0 Turn left at the junction with the San Juan Loop Trail.

8.0 Arrive in the San Juan Loop parking lot and your shuttle.

⑨ El Cariso Nature Trail

This short interpretive hike allows visitors to learn about the region's flora. The hike provides viewpoints and is a great trail for beginners, families, and those with only a little time to spend in the forest.

Distance: 1.2-mile loop
Approximate hiking time: 1 hour
Difficulty: Easy
Elevation gain: 125 feet
Trail surface: Spot gravel and dirt trail
Best season: Winter through spring; evenings or mornings in summer
Other trail users: Dogs
Canine compatibility: Leashed

dogs permitted
Fees and permits: Adventure Pass required
Maps: TOPO! CD: California CD 10; USGS: Alberhill
Trail contacts: Cleveland National Forest, Trabuco Ranger District, 1147 East Sixth Street, Corona 92879; (951) 736-1811; www.fs .fed.us/r5/cleveland

---

Finding the trailhead: Take Interstate 15 south from Riverside and exit at Central Avenue/Highway 74 in Lake Elsinore. Turn right onto Central Avenue/Highway 74 and drive 0.1 mile. Turn right onto Collier Avenue and drive 0.5 mile. Turn left at Riverside Drive and travel 3.2 miles. Veer left onto Grand Avenue and continue for 0.6 mile. Turn right onto Ortega Highway and continue into the mountains for 5.15 miles. Turn right onto South Main Divide Road (formerly Killeen Road). Drive 0.5 mile to the turnoff for El Cariso Visitor Center and Trail. The trail starts behind the visitor center. GPS: N33 38.55 / W117 24.36

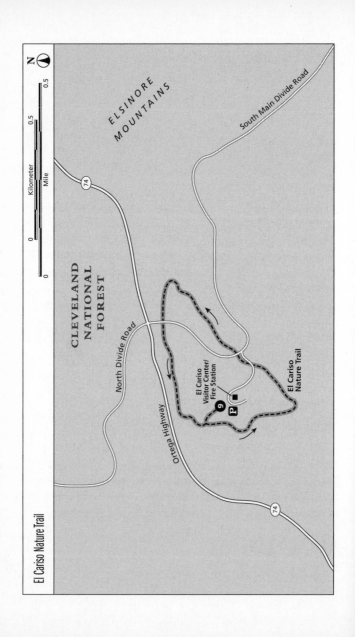

The Hike

The hike begins at the recently rebuilt El Cariso Visitor Center. There are some wonderful exhibits inside, and anyone taking this hike should first pay a visit to the center. Knowledgeable staff can provide answers to almost any question. Grab a copy of the brochure, which allows hikers to take a self-guided walk along the nature trail. The trail itself is a good way to get some quick exercise and learn about the native chaparral that is common in the region.

After hiking the trail, you should be able to recognize and name several different plants and their uses, including: manzanita, buckwheat, sage, scrub oak, sugarbush, and chamise. Wildflowers blossom along the trail in season, including poppies, black mustard, monkeyflower, and blue-eyed grass. Spring is the best time to visit, but the trail is lovely any time of year. Summer days tend to be hot, though.

The trail begins toward the southwest amidst a veritable crop of miner's lettuce. It is easy to tell where to go—just follow the numbers and the pamphlet. The route traverses below some wonderful, shady oak trees and then climbs easily up to a prominent overlook. The view encompasses some private land holdings within the national forest.

Here the trail flattens and heads eastward, ambling beside the remnants of a defunct mine. The trail crosses South Main Divide Road and moves through a landscape of Coulter pine, oak, and cypress trees before circling back westward to the visitor center and the trailhead.

Miles and Directions

0.0 Start at the trailhead behind El Cariso Visitor Center.

0.1 Reach the overlook and begin hiking east.

0.5 Cross South Main Divide Road.

0.9 Cross South Main Divide Road to the west.

1.2 Arrive back at the trailhead.

10 **Bear Canyon**

Sky-high views and solitude are the biggest rewards on this wonderful introductory trip into the San Mateo Wilderness. The trail is a jumping-off point for longer hike.

Distance: 4.8 miles out and back

Approximate hiking time: 2.5 hours

Difficulty: Easy

Elevation gain: 700 feet

Trail surface: Dirt trail, dirt road

Best season: Fall through spring; evenings or mornings in summer

Other trail users: Dogs

Canine compatibility: Leashed dogs permitted

Fees and permits: Adventure Pass required

Maps: TOPO! CD: California CD 10; USGS: Alberhill

Trail contacts: Cleveland National Forest, Trabuco Ranger District, 1147 East Sixth Street, Corona 92879; (951) 736-1811; www.fs .fed.us/r5/cleveland

Finding the trailhead: Take Interstate 15 south from Riverside and exit at Central Avenue/Highway 74 in Lake Elsinore. Turn right onto Central Avenue/Highway 74 and drive 0.1 mile. Turn right onto Collier Avenue and drive 0.5 mile. Turn left at Riverside Drive and travel 3.2 miles. Veer left onto Grand Avenue and continue for 0.6 mile. Turn right onto Ortega Highway and continue into the mountains for 8.3 miles. Park on the right side of the roadway in the San Juan Loop parking area. Cross the highway and start on the Bear Canyon Trail by the Ortega Country Cottage Candy Store and Gift Shoppe. GPS: N33 36.44 / W117 25.35

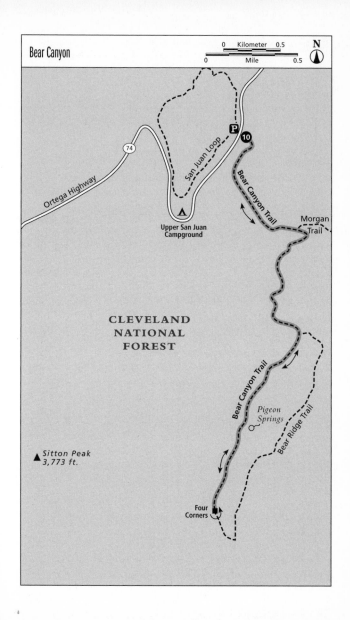

Bear Canyon

Ortega Highway

74

San Juan Loop

P 10

Bear Canyon Trail

Upper San Juan
Campground

Morgan
Trail

CLEVELAND
NATIONAL
FOREST

Bear Canyon Trail

Pigeon
Springs

Bear Ridge Trail

▲ Sitton Peak
3,773 ft.

Four
Corners

0   Kilometer   0.5

0   Mile   0.5

N

The Hike

This trail ascends from the same starting point as the heavily used San Juan Loop Trail. However, the entrance is located on the east side of the highway. As a consequence, it is often overlooked, giving it a great edge in serenity and solitude over other trails in the region. The route climbs and scrambles alongside lovely Bear Canyon, twisting across sage and coastal scrub–covered hillsides for a little over 0.5 mile. Here the trail intersects the even less-frequented Morgan Trail beneath a beautiful oak-covered arbor.

There isn't a lot of shade on the trail overall, but in certain sections the feel is decidedly arboreal. After the intersection, the trail climbs once again, arriving at a four-way crossing. The route is very well marked with signs located all along the way and is easily decipherable at every junction. Take the Bear Canyon Trail to the right, and follow the old dirt road to the shaded sylvan splendor of Pigeon Springs. This heavily wooded area is covered in lush oaks and shrubbery. A year-round water supply at the spring—a rarity this low in the Southern California mountains—provides the natural irrigation for this lovely slice of forest. The spring provides much-needed sustenance to the area's flora and fauna, but be sure to filter the water before human consumption. Pigeon Springs is a placid and lovely spot for a rest and picnic; it is also the turnaround point for this hike.

Options: Those with more energy may want to continue climbing another 0.5 mile to Four Corners—a historic trail junction that affords incredible views. Others may wish to take the Bear Canyon Loop, which includes the higher and drier Bear Ridge Trail. These options, while not overly burdensome, add more distance, difficulty, and elevation to the overall hike and will push it out of the easy range.

Miles and Directions

0.0 Start at the San Juan Loop Trail parking lot. Cross the highway to the trailhead, which is signed for Bear Canyon and San Mateo Wilderness.

0.6 Enter a lovely wooded grove before intersecting the Morgan Trail.

0.8 Turn right at the signed intersection with the Morgan Trail.

1.8 Turn right at the intersection with the Bear Canyon (formerly Verdugo Truck Trail) and Bear Ridge Trails. Follow the wide road into lovely wooded Pigeon Springs.

2.4 Arrive at Pigeon Springs; retrace your steps.

4.8 Arrive back at the trailhead.

Santa Rosa Plateau Ecological Preserve

The Santa Rosa Plateau is the verdant gemstone of Riverside County. Loaded with history and beauty, the preserve is a haven for rare endemic and endangered species. Geologically speaking, the plateau is a rarity in that it contains most of the state's remaining vernal pools. A volcanic remnant of hardened basalt lava, the region has been protected for posterity and presents a unique hiking experience in Southern California.

The preserve is strikingly beautiful, loaded with wildlife, and intriguing on many levels due to its historical, ecologic, and geologic attributes. It truly has something for everyone. Young and old can enjoy the trails of the Santa Rosa Plateau, and those wishing to make an epic trans-preserve hike can string together a variety of trails for an all-day outing. There are areas for equestrians, mountain bikers, hikers, and runners. Because of the preserve's sensitive nature, no pets are allowed; and due to the lack of dogs, wildlife is abundant.

Located on the southeastern arm of the Santa Ana Mountains, the plateau is home to many different native plant communities, including Engelmann oak woodlands and bunchgrass prairie. The oldest surviving buildings in Riverside County are located within the preserve and can be reached via several easy hiking routes. Docents lead guided tours on weekends through many regions of the park and can provide scads of information on the history and ecology of the preserve.

The type of landscape found in the preserve was once very common in the Southern California Basin. Unfortunately, flat-topped regions were also ideal for housing subdivisions, which have ultimately replaced the natural setting with a manufactured one. Visiting the Santa Rosa Plateau is like taking a walk through the past. The flora, fauna, and geology are all highly reminiscent of what was once common throughout the Southland.

The preserve is best experienced in late winter through spring, when the greens are vibrant after rains and the plateau is brimming with life. The preserve has an interactive visitor center, a well-informed staff, and miles of well-marked, highly frequented trails, most highlighting points of interest.

11 Vernal Pool Trail

A spectacular family adventure awaits on this very easy hike to a geologic rarity. The picturesque and idyllic vernal pool teems with life.

Distance: 1.2 miles out and back
Approximate hiking time: 1 hour
Difficulty: Easy
Elevation gain: 10 feet
Trail surface: Dirt trail
Best season: Spring; pool possibly dry at other times of the year
Other trail users: People in wheelchairs
Canine compatibility: No dogs allowed

Fees and permits: Day-use fee
Maps: TOPO! CD: California CD 10; USGS: Wildomar
Trail contacts: Santa Rosa Plateau Ecological Preserve, 39400 Clinton Keith Road, Murrieta 92562; (951) 677-6951; www .riversidecountyparks.org/park-directory/all-parks/santa-rosa-plateau

Finding the trailhead: From Riverside take Interstate 215 south to Murrieta. Exit at Clinton Keith Road and turn right. Drive west for 8 miles and stay straight as the road merges with Tenaja Road. After 2 more miles veer left onto Via Volcano, and follow it for just under a mile. Park at the well-marked trailhead on the east side of the road. GPS: N33 30.32 / W117 17.39

The Hike

The Vernal Pool Trail is without a doubt the most visited section of the Santa Rosa Plateau—and with good reason. Not only is it spectacularly beautiful, but it also contains the only example of a basalt-based vernal pool in Southern California. The plateau ridge provides wide-open vistas of the local mountains. The pool itself, when completely full, is stunning

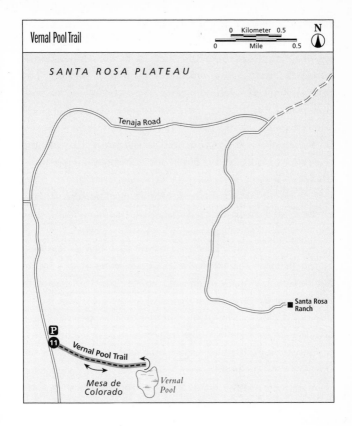

Vernal Pool Trail

SANTA ROSA PLATEAU

Tenaja Road

Santa Rosa
Ranch

Vernal Pool Trail

Mesa de
Colorado

Vernal
Pool

and incredibly picturesque. There are additional vernal pools in the region, but none of the others are accessible.

The vernal pool provides a record of the geologic history of Southern California. Ten million years ago, magma flows covered much of Riverside and Orange Counties. The basalt mesas that make up the Santa Rosa Plateau are the remnants of this ancient lava, and many such pools were created over time by tiny amounts of water amassing on the surface of the flat plain. These tiny pools of water evntually merged, forming large indentations that would fill up with seasonal rains and then disappear with the dry season—hence the term *vernal,* from the Latin for "spring." The pools have developed a distinctive ecosystem full of both flora and fauna that rely on this unique cycle of drought and deluge.

Creatures such as the Santa Rosa Plateau fairy shrimp are endemic only to the pools of this plateau. Fairy shrimp exist for most of their lives in suspended animation. They live in minuscule cysts that look like eggs but are actually embryos in a phase called diapause. In their cyst form, they can survive all sorts of extremes, and it's reported that cysts as old as 10,000 years have hatched after being placed in water. When water returns to the pool, some of the shrimp hatch. Others remain in diapause in case there isn't enough rainfall for the hatched shrimp to complete their reproductive cycle, thus ensuring survival of the species. These creatures live their entire life sequence in forty to fifty days; the remaining population exists only as cysts waiting for the next succession of rains.

The fairy shrimp are difficult to see and live only for a short while after the pool forms. Other creatures are more readily visible, such as the Pacific tree frog, western toad, and two-striped garter snake. The garter snakes can dart on and off the trail, which can be quite startling, but they are not harmful to humans. They feed on tadpoles and other small life-forms in and around the pool. Rattlesnakes are also common, though, so be on the lookout.

The flora on the trail is quite amazing. The plateau is one of the best examples of bunchgrass prairie remaining in California. Springtime blossoms include blue dicks, bush lupine, poppies, brodiaea, chocolate lilies, goldfields, and larkspur. Flowers bloom along the edges of the pool, and as the pool percolates and evaporates in the hot sun, the blooms will move inward, leaving concentric circles of flowers and blossoms.

The hike is a short one, perfect for children and even accessible to wheelchairs. Although rocky in spots, the trail is well maintained. The way is wide and broad, and the corridor to the pool is easy to navigate.

Miles and Directions

0.0 Start at the trailhead off Via Volcano, and begin hiking east on the Vernal Pool Trail.

0.5 Get a first glimpse of the pool from the top of a small hill.

0.6 Reach the pool and walkway. Benches and interpretive signs adorn the boardwalk. Retrace your steps.

1.2 Arrive back at the trailhead.

12 Historic Adobe Trail

Follow Adobe Creek through an idyllic glen, and hike through historic ranchlands to the oldest standing structures in Riverside County. The pastoral landscape is rustic and stunning.

Distance: 4.0 miles out and back
Approximate hiking time: 2 hours
Difficulty: Easy
Elevation gain: 300 feet
Trail surface: Dirt trail, dirt road
Best season: Spring; days exceedingly hot in summer
Other trail users: None
Canine compatibility: No dogs allowed

Fees and permits: Day-use fee
Maps: TOPO! CD: California CD 10; USGS: Wildomar
Trail contacts: Santa Rosa Plateau Ecological Preserve, 39400 Clinton Keith Road, Murrieta 92562; (951) 677-6951; www .riversidecountyparks.org/park-directory/all-parks/santa-rosa-plateau

Finding the trailhead: From Riverside take Interstate 215 south to Murrieta. Exit at Clinton Keith Road and turn right. Drive west for 9.9 miles, and stay straight as the road merges with Tenaja Road. The parking area for the Hidden Valley trailhead, which leads to the Historic Adobe, Coyote, and other trails, is on the left side of the road. Sylvan Meadows Multi-Use Area is on the right. GPS: N33 31.39 / W117 16.55

The Hike

Starting on the Coyote Trail, a gentle climb heads southward and into the rolling hills of the Santa Rosa Plateau. The route follows old roads and trails used by cattle ranchers dating back to the early 1800s. The region is very well

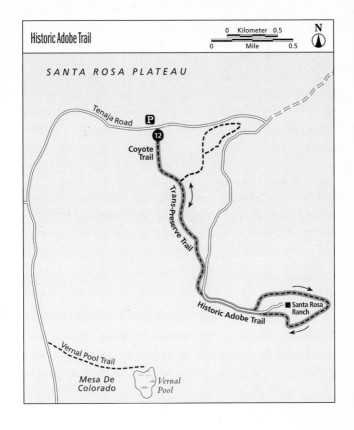

Historic Adobe Trail

SANTA ROSA PLATEAU

Tenaja Road

P

12

Coyote Trail

Trans-Preserve Trail

Historic Adobe Trail

Santa Rosa Ranch

Vernal Pool Trail

Mesa De Colorado

Vernal Pool

signed, almost too well signed, and there are many overlapping trails that can lead to the same location. In some ways this makes the trail signs a bit confusing. Although there isn't much chance for getting lost, unplanned exploration is a distinct possibility on the preserve.

With that in mind, it is a good idea to pick up a trail map at the visitor center before setting off on a hike. This route follows the Coyote Trail to the Trans-Preserve Trail, to the Adobe Trail, to the Adobe Loop Trail, to the Lomas Trail, back to the Adobe Trail, and out on the same return path. It is possible to make any number of changes, extended loops, or side ventures; and you can tailor the trail to suit any number of needs. Following this route, however, is the simplest way to see the old structures; the scenery is breath-taking as well.

After entering the Trans-Preserve Trail, the hike descends through a lovely valley alongside a seasonal creek. The trail undulates over another hill and past a bucolic outpost from the region's glory days of ranching, complete with corral and windmill. Make the creek crossing on the not-so-sturdy wood and metal bridge, and continue beyond several smaller trail crossings.

The adobes come into view, along with the lush green-ery and ancient trees surrounding them. The trail becomes an even wider road leading downward toward the historic buildings. Turn left at the junction with the Adobe Trail. The buildings, charming in their rural simplicity, date from 1846, when California was still part of Mexico and Spain. They served as bunkhouses for cowboys and vaqueros working on the ranch until the 1960s. The smaller one is even rumored to have been a holding cell for rowdy cow-hands who had imbibed a bit beyond their limits. Bars on the window seem to lend credence to such tales. There is much to explore around the adobes, and improvement plans are in the works. An enormous 300-year-old oak shades the entire area and makes a great spot for a rest and a picnic.

After exploring, continue east along the trail beyond the adobes. In less than 0.5 mile turn right onto the Adobe Loop Trail. Hike down into the wooded streambed where waters flow throughout a good portion of the year. Enjoy the splendor but watch out for poison oak, which is pervasive along the creek. Return to where the Lomas Trail meets the Loop Trail, and turn left back toward the adobes. Return via the same trail system to the trailhead.

Miles and Directions

0.0 Start at the Hidden Valley trailhead parking lot, and begin hiking south and uphill on the Coyote Trail.

0.4 Stay straight; then turn right at the junction onto the Trans-Preserve Trail.

0.7 Cross the creek on the metal and wood bridge. Stay on the Trans-Preserve Trail and follow the Historic Adobes signs.

1.2 Turn left onto the Historic Adobe Trail.

1.6 Arrive at the adobes.

2.0 Turn left onto the Adobe Creek Loop.

2.5 Turn left at the junction with the Lomas Trail, and return toward the adobes.

2.6 Turn right at the junction with the Historic Adobe Trail; retrace your steps to the trailhead.

4.0 Arrive back at the parking area.

13 Coyote–Oak Tree Trails

Visit rare Engelmann oaks in their natural setting on the Santa Rosa Plateau as you enjoy this creekside walk and the lovely hillsides.

Distance: 2.0-mile lollipop
Approximate hiking time: 1 hour
Difficulty: Easy
Elevation gain: 150 feet
Trail surface: Dirt trail, dirt road
Best season: Spring; days exceedingly hot in summer
Other trail users: None
Canine compatibility: No dogs allowed

Fees and permits: Day-use fee
Maps: TOPO! CD: California CD 10; USGS: Wildomar
Trail contacts: Santa Rosa Plateau Ecological Preserve, 39400 Clinton Keith Road, Murrieta 92562; (951) 677-6951; www .riversidecountyparks.org/park-directory/all-parks/santa-rosa-plateau

Finding the trailhead: From Riverside take Interstate 215 south to Murrieta. Exit at Clinton Keith Road and turn right. Drive west for 9.9 miles, and stay straight as the road merges with Tenaja Road. The parking area for the Hidden Valley trailhead, which leads to the Historic Adobe, Coyote, and other trails, is on the left side of the road. Sylvan Meadows Multi-Use Area is on the right. GPS: N33 31.39 / W117 16.55

The Hike

Starting on the Coyote Trail from the Hidden Valley trailhead, take the gentle climb heading southward toward the rolling hills and native grasslands that dominate the Santa Rosa Plateau. In 0.4 mile the trail reaches a T junction with the Trans–Preserve Trail. Turn left and head northeasterly

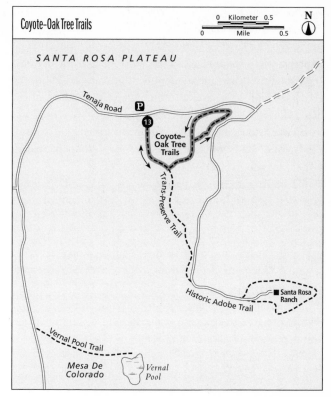

SANTA ROSA PLATEAU

Tenaja Road

🅿

13

Coyote–
Oak Tree
Trails

Trans-Preserve Trail

Historic Adobe Trail

■ Santa Rosa
Ranch

Vernal Pool Trail

Mesa De
Colorado

*Vernal
Pool*

toward the road and the Oak Tree loop. In another 0.2 mile the trail comes to a fork. Veer right onto the Oak Tree Trail, and descend into a lovely brookside vale where enormous stands of endangered Engelmann oak intertwine and tower above and alongside the path.

Engelmann oaks are endemic to Southern California and the northernmost reaches of Baja California. The ideal habitat for the trees is atop flat mesas, which unfortunately has conflicted with model locations for human habitation and tract homes. The trees have lost the battle with the ever-increasing population in the region, and sadly this grove remains as one of the only protected populations in existence. It is estimated that up to 70 percent of the oaks remaining in San Diego County were destroyed in the Cedar Fire of 2004, and housing along the foothills of the San Gabriel Mountains has virtually wiped out the oaks in their northernmost range. Other specimens do survive throughout the Southland, and there are groups vested in preserving and protecting this rare species.

These striking trees have a scaly gray bark, and the leaves are hued in gray, blue, and green. A motley mix of limbs radiate from the center of the large trunk and spread out to create a wild tentacle-like canopy. Many of the trees are very old—at least in human terms—with ages spanning 300 years. Walking among the trees carries an air of solemnity, and in some sense the trees retain a certain fairylike character, not unlike the magical forests of fantasy novels. Truly, a walk among these oaks is a walk through California's past, and that feeling is almost tangible.

The creek and its environs are of great interest, too, Wildflowers blossom in springtime profusion. Small pools, or tenajas, collect water that gives life to toads, frogs, turtles, and many other creatures that make their homes on the plateau. Coyotes frequent the hillsides and are so accustomed to seeing humans that they do not flee when seen. Circle the loop and return via the Coyote Trail.

Miles and Directions

0.0 Start by hiking south on the Coyote Trail from the Hidden Valley trailhead.

0.4 Turn left at the fork onto the Trans-Preserve Trail.

0.6 Take the right fork and descend into the Oak Tree Trail loop.

1.3 Return to the Trans-Preserve Trail and head back to the Coyote Trail. Turn right onto Coyote.

2.0 Arrive back at the Hidden Valley trailhead.

Agua Tibia
Wilderness

The Agua Tibia Wilderness is a lightly visited desert landscape on the edge of the Palomar Mountains. The region is marked with jagged canyons, tall peaks, and seasonal streams that have carved massive canyons down the dry mountain walls. The wilderness area is one of the few remaining examples of old-growth chaparral. There has been no fire in parts of this area for centuries, leaving massive stands of manzanita and red shank that have grown more than 20 feet high.

Pools created by the seasonal water that flows through the angular canyons led to the area's Spanish name, which means warm water. During springtime after heavy rains, the region is a veritable gold mine of wildflowers. Summertime temperatures can be scorching, often exceeding triple digits. Those visiting this rugged area would do well to do so on a cool day, when the afternoon temperatures are not likely to soar.

14 Dripping Springs Trail

Climb a ridge to gain expansive views of the highest mountains in Southern California.

Distance: 3.6 miles out and back
Approximate hiking time: 2 hours
Difficulty: Easy
Elevation gain: 1,200 feet
Trail surface: Dirt trail
Best season: Late fall through winter; avoid daytime in summer
Other trail users: Dogs, horses
Canine compatibility: Leashed dogs permitted

Fees and permits: Adventure Pass required for parking
Maps: TOPO! CD: California CD 10; USGS: Vail Lake
Trail contacts: Cleveland National Forest, Palomar Ranger District, 1634 Black Canyon Road, Ramona 92065; (760) 788-0250; www.fs.fed.us/r5/cleveland

Finding the trailhead: From Riverside take Interstate 215/15 south to Temecula. Exit onto Highway 79 east and drive 10 miles to Dripping Springs Campground. Turn right into the campground area and park almost immediately in the parking area signed for the Dripping Springs Trail. GPS: N33 27.49 / W116 58.18

The Hike

The Dripping Springs Trail is the main gateway into the Agua Tibia Wilderness, a wild and open landscape situated at the northern end of the Palomar Mountains. Much of the landscape is covered in chaparral that hasn't burned in more than a century. This hike samples some of that wilderness by hiking to a prominent ridgeline high above the surrounding countryside. Attempting this hike in summer or on a hot day is not advisable—there is no shade, and the constant sun

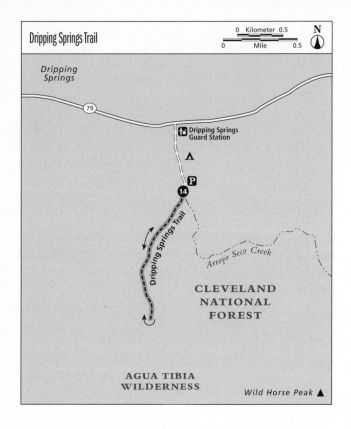

can be unbearable, even incapacitating. Making this hike in winter, however, can be downright refreshing.

The trail starts just before the campground and immediately crosses Arroyo Seco Creek. In rainy periods the water flows heavily, but Arroyo Seco means "dry creek" in Spanish, and the winter rains do not last long in this desert environment. Almost immediately the trial intersects the Wild Horse/Agua Tibia Wilderness Trail. Continue right, and begin hiking toward the ridgeline above.

From the outset, the trail climbs and climbs higher and higher into the mountains. It is steep but gentle, and the rewards are many. As the trail ascends, all of Southern California comes into view, starting with the Temecula area and Vail Lake. Eventually, breathtaking views of Santiago Peak, Mount Baldy, San Gorgonio, San Jacinto, the Desert Divide, the Pacific Ocean, Palomar Mountain, and nearly every other distinguishable feature one can think of appear on the horizon.

A spectacular jungle of aged chaparral shows just what the plant life of Southern California is capable of. Chamise, ceanothus, tree poppy, buckwheat, ribbonwood, and manzanita all grow trailside. Some absolutely gigantic and ancient examples of manzanita and ribbonwood, both living and dead, tower over portions of the route.

Generally a trail gaining this much elevation would be regarded as moderate in difficulty, but the short distance factors in here to make this trail a wonderful outing that can be accomplished by almost any hiker.

Miles and Directions

- **0.0** Start at the parking lot, and begin hiking on the roadway south toward the campground.
- **0.4** Enter the signed trailhead for Dripping Springs; sign the register on the left.
- **0.5** Cross Arroyo Seco Creek.
- **0.6** Enter the Agua Tibia Wilderness, and head right at the junction with the Wild Horse Trail.

1.1 Reach a viewpoint above the canyon.

1.2 Begin hiking through large patches of tall chaparral.

1.8 Gain a high ridge and magnificent clear-day views of Southern California. Return via the same route.

3.6 Arrive back at the trailhead.

San Jacinto Mountains–San Bernardino National Forest

The San Jacinto Mountains are the second-highest range in Southern California after the San Bernardinos. Their north–south orientation, towering pines, granite formations, magical vistas, and beautiful trails remind many visitors of the mountains' northern cousin, the Sierra Nevada. The San Jacinto Range shares much in common with the Range of Light: tall peaks, precipitous canyons, and an alpine environment that descends into desert in the east. The main differences between the two ranges are size and annual precipitation. In these arenas the San Jacinto Mountains cannot compare in magnitude with California's most glorious peaks. However, what these summits and ridges lack in size, they make up for in beauty and contrast. Views from ridgelines are some of the most magnificent anywhere. Best of all, the mountains are just a short drive from Riverside's city limits.

Administered by the San Bernardino National Forest, the mountains encompass a variety of ecosystems, and trails within the range vary from desert to pine forest. Most visitors to the mountains enter through Idyllwild or the Palm Springs Aerial Tramway, leaving large swaths of forest relatively unfrequented.

15 Suicide Rock

Hike to a lovely viewpoint in the San Jacinto Mountains overlooking the less than subtly named Suicide Rock.

Distance: 5.5 miles out and back
Approximate hiking time: 2.5 hours
Difficulty: Moderate
Elevation gain: 2,000 feet
Trail surface: Dirt trail
Best season: Year-round
Other trail users: None
Canine compatibility: No dogs allowed
Fees and permits: Adventure Pass required for parking. A wilderness permit is required for hiking and can be picked up at the Idyllwild Ranger Station.
Maps: TOPO! CD: California CD 10; USGS: San Jacinto Peak
Trail contacts: San Bernardino National Forest, San Jacinto Ranger District, 54270 Pinecrest (mailing address: P.O. Box 518) Idyllwild 92549; (909) 382-2921; www.fs.fed.us/r5/sanbernardino

Finding the trailhead: From Riverside take Highway 60 east until it merges with Interstate 10 to Banning. Exit onto Eighth Street/Highway 243 and turn right. Make the first left onto Lincoln and drive east for 0.5 mile. Turn right onto Highway 243 and follow it into the mountains for 23.6 miles. Park in the dirt parking area across from Idyllwild Park. GPS: N33 45.9 / W116 43.18

The Hike

This hike follows the Deer Springs Trail through the grandly forested San Jacinto Mountains. It begins at the trailhead located on Highway 243 just outside Idyllwild. The trip is uphill for the entire route and gains a good amount of eleva-

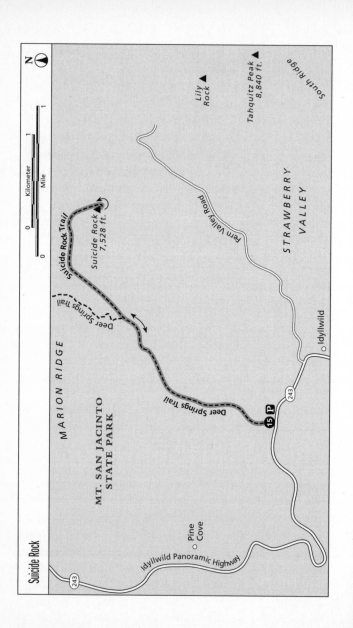

Suicide Rock

tion, but the gradient is rather gentle, and the scenery is like the mountain town below, idyllic.

The actual trailhead is not easy to spot from the parking lot, and many people have inadvertently cut little paths to the main trail. Pick one and it will lead to the trail within a minute or so of walking time. Like most of the higher reaches of the San Jacinto Mountains, this trail is covered in lodgepole and Jeffrey pine; the towering trees loom overhead and provide ample shade even on warm summer afternoons. Large boulders dot the landscape, and wildlife is common, especially in the morning or evening. Quickly the route climbs away from the highway and urban noises, ambling northeasterly through a peaceful canyon. An intermittent brook babbles below the trail during rainier times and early in the season; but like most water sources in Riverside County, the brook dries up by midsummer.

After 1.5 miles the Deer Springs Trail intersects the signed spur trail for Suicide Rock. Take the right fork and ascend the remaining 1.25 miles to the overlook. The drop-off and views are amazing. Tahquitz Peak and Lily Rock dominate the horizon, and vistas spread across Strawberry Valley and a good part of the Southern California landscape. Rock climbers sometimes scramble up the steep granite outcrop, so be careful not to dislodge loose rocks along the edges—and be mindful of the edge.

The area is ripe with native legend. According to Cahuilla mythos, two young lovers leapt to their death after their parents forbade their affection. Their jump bequeathed the rock its somber sobriquet. In addition to this Native American version of Romeo and Juliet is the legend of the demonlike Tahquish. An angry and powerful god, he prowled this region of the forest looking for young maidens and the unwary. All who disappeared in the region were said to have been devoured by his ferocious maw.

From the overlook, be sure to make the short climb to the top of the conical peak, which sits at 7,528 feet above sea level. Sign the summit register, and then return via the Deer Springs Trail.

Miles and Directions

0.0 Start at the trailhead and begin hiking on the Deer Springs Trail.

1.5 Turn right at the junction with the Suicide Rock Trail.

2.6 Arrive at Suicide Rock overlook.

2.7 Reach the summit. Retrace your steps.

5.5 Arrive back at the Deer Springs trailhead.

16 Ernie Maxwell Scenic Trail

Hike through a peaceful forest, crossing streams on an easy trail suited for families. This is a good hike for those interested in botany—many species of trees, shrubs, and wildflowers can be observed along the trail.

Distance: 5.0 miles out and back

Approximate hiking time: 1.5 hours

Difficulty: Easy

Elevation gain: 600 feet

Trail surface: Dirt trail

Best season: Year-round

Other trail users: Horses, dogs, bicycles

Canine compatibility: Leashed dogs permitted

Fees and permits: Adventure Pass required for parking

Maps: TOPO! CD: California CD 10; USGS: San Jacinto Peak

Trail contacts: San Bernardino National Forest, San Jacinto Ranger District, 54270 Pinecrest (mailing address: P.O. Box 518) Idyllwild 92549; (909) 382-2921; www.fs.fed.us/r5/sanbernardino

Finding the trailhead: Take Interstate 215 south from Riverside and exit at Case Road/Highway 74 east toward Hemet. Drive 31.6 miles to the Mountain Center junction with Highway 243. Veer left onto Highway 243 and drive north for 4 miles. Turn right onto Saunders Meadow Road and follow it as it curves and turns for 1.5 miles. Turn right onto Pine Avenue. In 0.1 mile turn right onto Tahquitz View Drive. The trailhead is located on the right about 0.75 mile from where Tahquitz Meadow Drive becomes a dirt road. GPS: N33 45.53 / W116 41.15

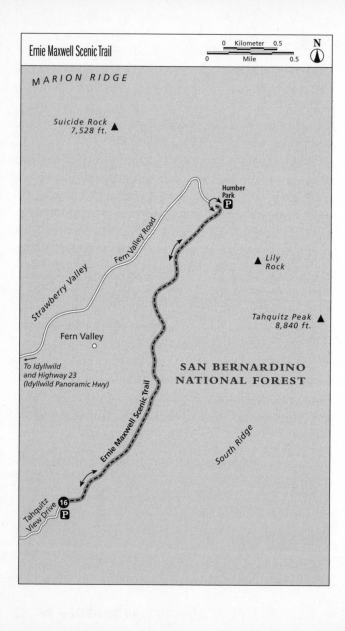

Ernie Maxwell Scenic Trail

MARION RIDGE

Suicide Rock
7,528 ft. ▲

Humber
Park
🅿

Strawberry Valley

Fern Valley Road

▲ Lily
Rock

Fern Valley ○

Tahquitz Peak ▲
8,840 ft.

To Idyllwild
and Highway 23
(Idyllwild Panoramic Hwy)

SAN BERNARDINO
NATIONAL FOREST

Ernie Maxwell Scenic Trail

South Ridge

Tahquitz
View Drive
16 🅿

0   Kilometer   0.5

0   Mile   0.5

N

The Hike

The Ernie Maxwell Scenic Trail, named for the late Idyll-wild conservationist, is often proclaimed to be the best and easiest introduction to hiking in the Idyllwild region. This is certainly true—the trail's gentle elevation gain is spread out over 2.5 miles, making the uphill walk barely noticeable. Nestled under a lovely forest canopy of pine, cedar, and oak, the setting is sublime and shady. Several small creeks cross the trail and sustain the region's flora and fauna.

The trail sits just above the outskirts of town and just below the wilderness boundary, making this a best-of-both-worlds type of hike. Mountain bikes, dogs, and horses all frequent the trail. As the route approaches the turnaround point at Humber Park, wonderful views of both Lily Peak and Suicide Rock come into view. Humber Park has restrooms and picnic tables and is a nice spot for a lunch break before retracing your steps.

The hike out is just as nice as the hike in, except the way back is all downhill. The vantage differs on the way back. Some views open up that on a clear day, reach all the way to the Pacific Ocean. Take the time to explore and enjoy the different plants and trees that grow along the path. Many discoveries await.

This hike easily can be turned into a one-way downhill trip by parking one car at the trailhead and another at Humber Park. Almost anyone able to walk without difficulty should be able to handle the downhill trek.

Miles and Directions

0.0 Start at the trailhead on Tahquitz Meadow Drive, and begin hiking on the Ernie Maxwell Scenic Trail.

2.5 Arrive at Humber Park, a nice spot for a lunch break. Retrace your steps—this time downhill.

5.0 Arrive back at trailhead.

17 South Fork Trail (San Jacinto River)

This trail combines great views of the San Jacinto Mountains from a lovely promontory with a wonderful descent into a lush canyon, complete with wildlife and fishing opportunities.

Distance: 5.0 miles out and back

Approximate hiking time: 2.5 hours

Difficulty: Easy

Elevation gain: 1,100 feet

Trail surface: Dirt trail

Best season: Late winter through late spring

Other trail users: Horses, dogs

Canine compatibility: Leashed dogs permitted

Fees and permits: Adventure Pass required for parking

Maps: TOPO! CD: California CD 10; USGS: Blackburn Canyon

Trail contacts: San Bernardino National Forest, San Jacinto Ranger District, 54270 Pinecrest (mailing address: P.O. Box 518) Idyllwild 92549; (909) 382-2921; www.fs.fed.us/r5/sanbernardino

Finding the trailhead: Take Interstate 215 south from Riverside and exit at Case Road/Highway 74 east toward Hemet. Drive for 29.4 miles until just beyond the hairpin turn known as White Post. Turn and park on the right at the signed South Fork trailhead. GPS: N33 41.51 / W116 45.36

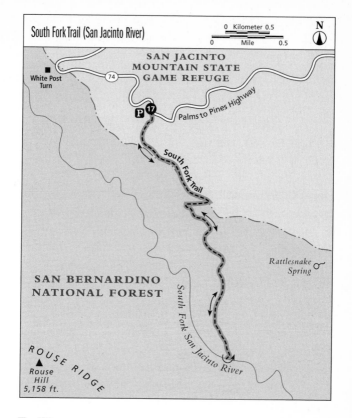

South Fork Trail (San Jacinto River)

0 Kilometer 0.5
0 Mile 0.5

N

SAN JACINTO
MOUNTAIN STATE
GAME REFUGE

White Post
Turn

74

P 17

Palms to Pines Highway

South Fork Trail

SAN BERNARDINO
NATIONAL FOREST

South Fork San Jacinto River

Rattlesnake
Spring

ROUSE RIDGE
Rouse
Hill
5,158 ft.

The Hike

From Highway 74 the South Fork Trail seems to be nothing but a turnout in the roadway, resembling little more than a hot, sparsely shaded route through chaparral. Absolutely nothing could be further from the truth. Although there is almost always a car or two parked at the trailhead, this gem of a hike it is not overcrowded like the more popular trails situated higher up in the forest.

Starting out along the high and precipitous crest of Rouse Ridge, views open up in all directions as the trail climbs gently but steadily up 500 feet in the first mile. The trail escapes the noise of the highway very quickly and feels untamed and savage almost from its outset. Since the route travels parallel to the canyon, the river below also rises in elevation as the trail heads upstream. At the top of the ridge, the trail descends gently for a mile before dropping rapidly, losing 500 feet in less than 0.25 mile.

Here the beauty of the San Jacinto's South Fork is more than evident; it is all encompassing. The area is slated for possible wilderness designation, and the big-cone Douglas fir trees complement the cottonwoods and willows that line the riverbanks. The scene appears more East Coast than Southern California desert. Many plant and animal species claim the streambanks as their home, including mountain lions and bald eagles.

Fishermen and hunters use the trail as well, but the area is a great place to enjoy the marvels of one of the only relatively wild rivers remaining in Riverside County. The dam at Lake Hemet does reduce the wildness of the South Fork because many other tributaries feed the river, giving it a vitality and lushness that is without compare.

Miles and Directions

0.0 Start at the signed South Fork trailhead and begin hiking south along the trail.

2.5 Arrive at the South Fork of the San Jacinto River. This is your turnaround point.

5.0 Arrive back at the trailhead.

18 Ramona Trail to Tool Box Spring

Hike up a lovely chaparral–covered mountainside to beautiful pine forests and an improved spring. Views of the surrounding countryside are spectacular.

Distance: 6.0 miles out and back
Approximate hiking time: 3 hours
Difficulty: Easy
Elevation gain: 1,600 feet
Trail surface: Dirt trail, dirt road
Best season: Late fall through late spring
Other trail users: Horses, dogs, bicycles
Canine compatibility: Leashed dogs permitted

Fees and permits: Adventure Pass required for parking
Maps: TOPO! CD: California CD 10; USGS: Anza
Trail contacts: San Bernardino National Forest, San Jacinto Ranger District, 54270 Pinecrest (mailing address: P.O. Box 518) Idyllwild 92549; (909) 382-2921; www.fs.fed.us/r5/sanbernardino

Finding the trailhead: Take Interstate 215 south from Riverside and exit at Case Road/Highway 74 east toward Hemet. Drive for 40.1 miles. Just before Morris Ranch Road, park in the large lot on the right. GPS: N33 37.16 / W116 38.2

The Hike

From Highway 74 in Garner Valley, hike almost 0.25 mile until the dirt road heading south becomes a singletrack trail and begins ambling its way higher and higher into the forest. The trail switchbacks numerous times, wandering along the contours of the countryside canyons that spread down from the long alluvial hogback of Thomas Mountain.

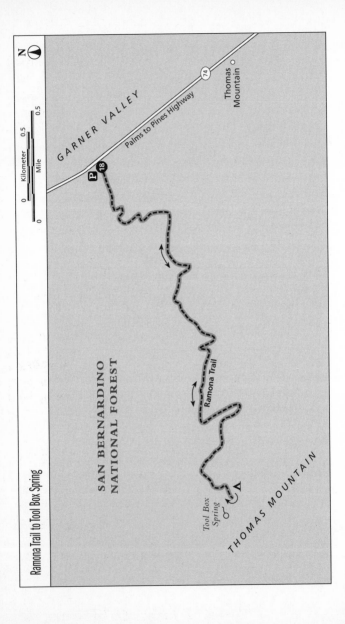

Ramona Trail to Tool Box Spring

The trail is wide open and not shaded from the sun until near the very highest reaches of the route. This is a perfect early-morning hike in summer or a great winter trek, but hot afternoons should be avoided. Gaining more than 1,500 feet of elevation from Garner Valley, this is one of the tougher hikes in this guide, but the gradient is gentle and steady. The trail definitely heads upward, but the climb is at a reasonable and nearly constant rate that makes it seem to be merely a walk up a hill. Breathtaking views open up at every turn.

Along the gentle incline, the hike passes through lovely coastal chaparral that includes toyon, manzanita, scrub oak, pitcher sage, climbing penstemon, chamise, black sage, and yucca. Various wildflowers blossom at differing times throughout the year, including lovely stands of golden California poppies, yerba santa, black mustard, and buckwheat.

As the route nears the top, it enters a mixed oak and pine forest and intersects a roadway just below Tool Box Spring. Turn left to see water from the improved spring coming out of a pipe and entering into a metal basin. Following the road a little farther leads to a lush, beautifully wooded yellow-pine island in the sky. Tool Box Spring Campground has several benches and is a wonderful spot to rest or enjoy a picnic before heading back down the mountain.

Miles and Directions

0.0 Start at the trailhead, and begin hiking south along the road up the hillside as it becomes the Ramona Trail.

0.2 Veer left off the dirt road and head up the singletrack Ramona Trail.

2.3 Enter a mixed oak and pine forest.

2.6 Veer left onto a dirt road.

2.8 Pass Tool Box Spring.

3.0 Reach Tool Box Spring Campground. Rest a spell or enjoy a picnic before heading back down the mountain.

6.0 Arrive back at the trailhead.

19 Cedar Springs Trail to Little Desert

Hike to the top of the lovely Desert Divide section of the lower San Jacinto Mountains to the junction with the Pacific Crest Trail. Views in all directions make this one of the most scenic places in all Southern California.

Distance: 5.0 miles out and back
Approximate hiking time: 2.5 hours
Difficulty: Easy
Elevation gain: 1,400 feet
Trail surface: Dirt trail
Best season: Late fall through late spring
Other trail users: Horses, dogs, bicycles
Canine compatibility: Leashed dogs permitted

Fees and permits: Adventure Pass required for parking
Maps: TOPO! CD: California CD 10; USGS: Palm View Peak
Trail contacts: San Bernardino National Forest, San Jacinto Ranger District, 54270 Pinecrest (mailing address: P.O. Box 518) Idyllwild 92549; (909) 382-2921; www.fs.fed.us/r5/sanbernardino

Finding the trailhead: Take Interstate 215 south from Riverside and exit at Case Road/Highway 74 east toward Hemet. Drive for 40.6 miles to Morris Ranch Road. Turn left onto Morris Ranch Road and drive 3.5 miles to the parking on the left. Walk up the road 0.1 mile to the trailhead. GPS: N33 39.10 / W116 35.23

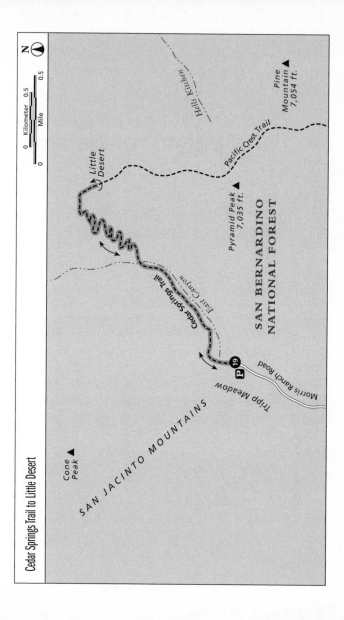

Cedar Springs Trail to Little Desert

The Hike

From the parking area, walk north up the road to the signed trailhead and enter the opening in the fence. For the first 1.0 mile the trail alternates between road and singletrack. There are several gates that must be opened and closed as the trail passes through private property. Thankfully it is open to the public, allowing access to this beautiful landscape. Please respect the land and the owners who graciously allow public access; follow posted guidelines, and make sure all gates are closed after you pass through.

The trail follows the road and a lovely sylvan creek through some grassy meadows and then enters a picnic area. From this rest spot, the trail snakes its way up the mountainside. The switchbacks are obvious from the trail, and the entire route to the top can be seen from the bottom. The 1.25 miles of trail leading to the Pacific Crest Trail (PCT) are uphill, but very gentle. This is perhaps the simplest way up to the famous route that works its way from Mexico to Canada.

Since the mountainside is south and west facing, the best time to get started is before the sun is high in the sky. The route is exposed to the sun, and temperatures quickly can reach scorching in the summertime. However, winter excursions and early jaunts are incredibly rewarding. In winter the westward views extend to the Pacific and the clear azure skies adorn the heavens.

Atop the crest, a solitary oak tree provides shade at the junction. From here turn right and follow the trail to the top of a not-so-noteworthy promontory designated as Little Desert on topographic maps. While the hill itself isn't significant for a named peak, the 360-degree vistas are. Everything from the Salton Sea, Coachella Valley, the mountains of San Diego, Los Angeles, and the islands off the Pacific Coast can be surveyed from on high.

One of the great things about this trail is that if you still have the energy, a number of side ventures can be made by striking out in any direction.

Miles and Directions

0.0 Start from the parking area, and work north on the road to the gated and signed entrance for the Cedar Springs Trail.

0.1 Pass through the gate to the right and close it behind you.

0.2 Walk along the roadway.

0.5 Pass through the gate and close it behind you.

0.7 Pass through the next gate and close it.

0.8 Arrive at the picnic table and meadow.

1.0 Begin hiking up the switchbacks to the Pacific Crest Trail.

2.25 Arrive at the Pacific Crest Trail. Turn right and proceed to the top of Little Desert.

2.5 Arrive at the top of Little Desert. Return via the same route.

5.0 Arrive back at the trailhead parking.

Anza-Borrego Desert State Park

Anza-Borrego Desert State Park is the largest state-owned parcel of parkland outside Alaska, making the park California's largest preserved area outside the National Park System. Anza-Borrego is infrequently visited due to its remoteness and desert climate, but its austere beauty is undeniable. Bordered by the Salton Sea; the Laguna, Cuyamaca, San Jacinto, and Santa Rosa Mountains; and San Diego and Riverside Counties, the park is nearly as large as the state of Rhode Island. A land of marked contrast, it is full of mountains, washes, and depressions. Desert wildflowers bring the most visitors to the region, and in years of heavy rainfall, the multihued blossoms are ubiquitous and enticing.

From high mountain ridges affording sunrise and sunset views unmatched anywhere else in the lower forty-eight states to ghostly ruins and Native American sites, the vast desert reaches of Anza-Borrego have much to offer.

20 Lookout Mountain via the Pacific Crest Trail

Hike a short distance to an isolated and rarely visited desert peak that offers great views on the way up and down. Springtime flowers are spectacular.

Distance: 1.9 miles out and back
Approximate hiking time: 1 hour
Difficulty: Easy
Elevation gain: 600 feet
Trail surface: Dirt trail
Best season: Late fall through late spring
Other trail users: Horses, dogs
Canine compatibility: Leashed dogs permitted

Fees and permits: Adventure Pass required for parking
Maps: TOPO! CD: California CD 10; USGS: Butterfly Peak
Trail contacts: Anza-Borrego Desert State Park, 200 Palm Canyon Drive, Borrego Springs 92004; (760) 767-5311; www.parks.ca.gov/?page_id=638

Finding the trailhead: Take Interstate 215 south from Riverside and exit at Case Road/Highway 74 east toward Hemet. Drive 45.8 miles to the parking area for the Pacific Crest Trail, 1.4 miles beyond Highway 391. GPS: N33 33.46 / W116 34.32

The Hike

From the large parking area for the Pacific Crest Trail (PCT), cross Highway 74 and follow the route southward toward Mexico. Pass through the gate, and follow the trail for 0.5 mile up to the ridgeline leading toward the summit. In another 0.2 mile the summit appears to the southeast.

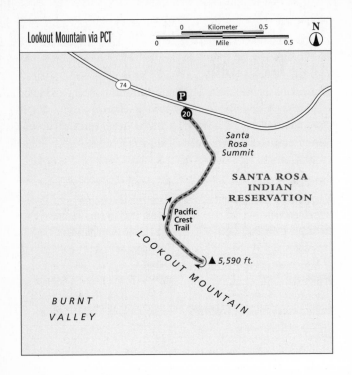

Look carefully for the firebreak on the left marked by a pile of rocks, also known as a cairn. It is easy to miss, so pay careful attention.

Turn left at the cairn and hike off the PCT onto a use trail. From here begin ascending toward the mountain. There are a few junctions with other firebreaks, but all are ducked with piles of rocks. The trail from this point may be a bit brushy. At times, bushwhacking may be required to continue toward the top. Continue upwards on a steeper incline, following the rock piles along the route. A bench located on the summit is a perfect spot to rest or to watch a kaleidoscope-like sunset.

There is a summit register on top where hikers can sign their names and philosophize or wax poetic. Popcorn flower and phacelia are common blooming species on the mountaintop during greener times. The summit itself is somewhat of a misnomer. The top is quite broad, flat, and full of shrubs. There are views, however. Sunrises and sunsets can be absolutely magical high above the desert, but the vistas are actually better along the way up and down.

The summit does provide ample opportunity for relaxation courtesy of the mystery bench. Take advantage of this great spot to reflect on a nice short hike atop a peaceful and beautiful desert mountain.

Miles and Directions

0.0 Start at the parking lot, and begin hiking southward on the Pacific Crest Trail.

0.6 Turn left and begin ascending the use trail to the top of Lookout Mountain.

0.9 Follow the rock cairns to stay on the use trail.

0.9 Arrive atop Lookout Mountain. Enjoy the views before retracing your steps.

1.8 Arrive back at the PCT parking lot.

About the Author

Allen Riedel is an award-winning photographer, author, and columnist. He is author of a biweekly column in the Outdoor section of the *Riverside Press Enterprise* as well as two hiking guidebooks: *100 Classic Hikes Southern California* and *Best Hikes with Dogs Southern California,* both published by The Mountaineers Books. He has also written three books in the Best Easy Day Hikes series: Riverside, San Bernardino, and an update for San Diego.

Allen is an English teacher for Val Verde Unified School District. He lives in Riverside with his wife, Monique; twin daughters, Sierra and Makaila; and son, Michael.